THE COLOUR ATLAS OF

WINE

THE COLOUR ATLAS OF

WINE

CHRISTOPHER FOULKES

ALL PHOTOGRAPHS SUPPLIED BY
CEPHAS PICTURE LIBRARY

PRINCIPAL PHOTOGRAPHER
MICK ROCK

SUNBURST BOOKS

THE COLOUR ATLAS OF WINE

Conceived and produced by
Segrave Foulkes Publishers and Malcolm Saunders Publishing Ltd., London

This edition published in 1995 by
Sunburst Books, Deacon House, 65 Old Church Street, London SW3 5BS

Picture on page one:
juice from these ripe Pinot Noir grapes from Verzenay will become champagne.

Picture on title pages:
vineyards in the Chianti Classico zone of Tuscany, Central Italy

Designed by Nigel O'Gorman
Edited by Carrie Segrave
Typesetting and page makeup by MacGuru
Illustrations by Trevor Lawrence
Maps by Cartographic Solutions Ltd
Photographs by Cephas Picture Library,
principal photographer Mick Rock

Maps on pages
35, 37, 41, 43, 56, 67, 73, 81, 87, 89, 92, 100,
103, 105, 111, 112, 117, 121, 123
based upon Mountain High Maps™
Copyright © 1993 Digital Wisdom, Inc.

ISBN 1 85778 081 7

Printed and bound in Hong Kong

CONTENTS

INTRODUCTION

THE CORK IS PULLED, with a satisfying noise. The wine glugs into the glass. Candlelight catches the gold of a fresh white, the ruby of a rich red. The aroma is enticing, the first sip keeps all the promises made by sight and smell. The first question anyone asks is 'where does that wine come from?'

Wine is about places. The names on the labels are place names, be they as broad as California or France, or as local as a single vineyard or farm. We use other names, those of the grapes that the wine is made from, or of its makers, but the talk about wine always comes back to places.

That is why this guide to wine is an atlas. It uses the maps to pinpoint where different wines come from in an attempt to bring some order to the profusion of names, labels and bottles.

Knowing where a wine comes from is the first step to knowing what it will taste like. Breaking the code comes next: the names and terms on the labels will, in return for a little homework, yield much insight into what's in that bottle.

Open the bottle, pour the wine, and prepare to enjoy.

FREEDOM TO CHOOSE

Few pleasures are as varied as wine. A good wine store has an amazing range of styles, flavours and colours. The only parallel is with a library, be it stocked with books or movies or computer software. This choice offers the freedom to browse, to experiment, to try a bottle with an odd name.

Like all freedoms, that of choice tends to wither if not used. If everyone who walks into a wine store demands Chardonnay, that is all the vineyards will plant and that is all we will get. Lovers of Riesling, Sémillon, Chenin Blanc and 500 other white grapes will face disappointment. As with old-fashioned apples, or breeds of cattle, we need to preserve the less obvious and the downright esoteric grape varieties.

Another risk old-established vineyards face is falling out of fashion. Wine drinkers tend to get to know a few big names, which is hard on the little ones in the backwoods. Wine traditionally carries its place-name on the label, which makes it possible to distinguish one area's produce from another. Let us go on trying the obscure, the novel and the traditional. If we do not, they will very soon vanish.

SHOULD WINE CARRY PASSPORTS?

The last few years have opened up the debate about why place matters. In broad terms, the argument is between the attitudes of the 'Old World' of wine — Europe — and the 'New': the Americas, Australasia, South Africa.

The lucky wine drinker is the beneficiary of this debate, which, working in parallel with new technology, has spurred on a dramatic rise in the quality of wine.

Very broadly, the Old World says that place matters most, and that the wine label should be like a passport, carrying the wine's place and date of birth. The New World argues that technique can and does override the contribution made by the site, soil and climate of the vineyard.

Can good wines now be made anywhere, thanks to technology? Is the type of grape used more important than the soil it is grown in? It used to be thought, believed, that the vineyard mattered above all. French wine law is built around

the principle that wines differ because they come from different places. And some places, decrees that law, are better than others. End of discussion. Thus in France a *grand cru* vineyard will always make better wine than an ordinary vineyard — or so the logic goes.

When vines were planted in the USA and Australia, no laws were on hand to define the *grands crus*. No-one *could* know where they were: time and trial show where, no science can really help. So the 'New World' vineyards are planted in the places chosen, sometimes at random and sometimes with a great deal of thought, by individuals.

Old World wine laws spell out not just the where, but the what and the how of wine growing. The grapes that can be grown, and the methods used to tend them and make the resulting wine, are written in the law of the land. In the New World, winemakers have had to satisfy broad rules about health, but otherwise how the wine is made has been entirely up to them.

But this is debate, not war; and, as in any good debate, both sides have learnt something in the process. The New World countries are in many instances formulating appellation rules defining just what should be in bottles which

Harvesting Cabernet Sauvignon grapes at Château Léoville-Barton in Bordeaux.

claim the name of the more successful areas, and where the boundaries of such areas are. The Old World has begun to take more note of the New World habit of labelling wine by its grape variety: you can now follow the performance of your favourite grape around the world as you might that of your favourite football team — see page 10.

The cross-fertilization goes further than the outward spread of the classic grape varieties, with investment, joint ventures, expertise, new technology and people being shared between continents: a happy thought, as many an Antipodean winemaker is proving, is that by shuttling between hemispheres, and therefore seasons, you can double your winemaking opportunities. The next debate, when all the current developments and trends have been assimilated, will be about how to avoid going too far, and losing local flavours and traditions.

In the end, it is that vital cork-pulling moment that matters: is the wine delicious? Is it a boost to the meal, the mood, the occasion? If not, it has failed: there are plenty more to try.

THE KEYS TO
WINE

W ine is there to be enjoyed. It can be as simple or
as complex a pleasure as you like. Simplicity is
when a straightforward bottle helps wash down an
everyday meal, or enlivens a gathering of friends.
Complexity is when you explore the enormous range of
wine tastes and nuances. Its enjoyment is not supposed
to be an obstacle course, beset by traps of protocol
and procedure. A few keys make it easier to enjoy
wine, be the pleasure sensual or cerebral. There are
ways of grouping wines: in style categories, by grapes,
by taste and flavour. There are practical knacks for
opening, decanting, serving and tasting. With wine, a
little knowledge can go a long way.

A Pinot Noir vine at Morey St-Denis in Burgundy.

CHOOSING WINE

THERE ARE TWO KINDS OF WINE: the ones you can afford, or are prepared to pay for, and the others. Price inhibits experiment: most people find themselves returning to a few safe names, all around the same price, because there are just too many wines out there to choose from.

Truly, the choice can be daunting. First there is price (it always comes first). Then colour, style, country of origin, grape, vineyard, winemaker....

This book is arranged around the places the wines come from: still the most fascinating, and informative, starting-point when considering the world of wine. But it could instead have considered grape varieties one by one, or devoted itself to listing all the foremost wine estates and makers around the world. Faced, then, with the 50 or so countries that make wine — and the ever-increasing numbers of them that want to export it to the rest of us — we need some ground rules. What are the types of wine?

COLOUR AND STYLE

Red and white — and don't forget rosé — are the first stage. Some, though, might best be described as 'brown': fortified ones mostly. Fortified? These are the wines which have spirits added during their making: sherry and port are the most famous examples. Then wine can be any of the three colours, and either still or sparkling. That exhausts the basic choices.

Wines can be sweet or dry, heavy or light, fresh with youth or redolent of maturity. Age at least is easy to judge: just look at the date on the label. If there is none, assume this is a wine to drink quickly.

DECODING THE LABEL

For further clues about wine style, consult the label — particularly the back label, if there is one. It may all be spelled out. Frustratingly, most European wines do not have back labels. You are supposed to gather the information about the wine from knowing the area from which it comes.

The words on the label may include any or all of the following: area of origin, vineyard and/or estate where the grapes were grown, grape variety used, and the name of the producer. The label may say, in the local language, if the wine

is sweet or dry (see page 31 for some of the key words). Some wines have a name: this may be a brand, made up by the maker, or a local style of wine. And there may also be an indication of quality level: *vin de table,* or *grand cru;* or a legal guarantee of its status such as VDQS.

GRAPE VARIETIES

Grape names are the modern answer to the puzzle of how to spot a wine's style (without opening the bottle). Winemakers in the New World of wine, especially California, seized upon the grape name as the clue to making a certain style of wine, then to selling it. If, they reasoned, the French make those fabulous white burgundies from the Chardonnay grape, the shortest route to an equally good if not better wine is to plant Chardonnay. In turn, the grape name on the label signals a certain style and taste to the buyer.

The French, whose grape varieties have been borrowed wholesale, find all this a bit over-simplified. There is much more to it than the grape, they counter. So there is, but the name of a grape is a useful starting point.

Wine people speak (and write) of the grapes and the wine they make in the same way, which can be confusing. Strictly speaking, Cabernet Sauvignon is a strain of grape vine, but the name is used for the vine's fruit and the wines made from it. We find the grape name usually attached to a place, with greater or lesser emphasis on the two facts. Thus the label or wine list may say 'Australian Chardonnay' or 'South African white' with the grapes in the smaller print.

The 'top six' varieties are profiled below — there are at least 1,000 more. Luckily only a few get their names on labels.

WHITE WINE GRAPES

■ *Chardonnay* is the most common name, having become the signal for a full, fruity, sometimes even slightly sweet wine. Chardonnay takes to the taste of oak ageing, acquiring enjoyable buttery hints. As well as white burgundy, it takes up a big part of the champagne vineyards and is grown virtually everywhere in the wine world. Chardonnay is so versatile that it has many styles: the one most often found, the rich butter-and-oak sort, is almost certainly a passing fashion.

■ *Sauvignon Blanc* made its name in the Loire, with Sancerre and Pouilly Fumé, then redoubled its fame with New Zealand Sauvignons: grassy, herby and even rich where the Loire wines suggest steel and flint. Bordeaux uses it a lot for white Graves and other wines: it blends well with Sémillon. Whether piercingly acidic or soft and blowsy, Sauvignon has a green, fruity style. It is rarely a wine to age.

■ *Riesling* is the grape of the great wines of Germany, Alsace and (increasingly) of parts of the New World. Unlike Sauvignon, it makes wines to keep. Rieslings, if well made, can last 30 or 40 years. Many start off sweet, but they age to dryness, while retaining a refreshing acidity. Young Rieslings smell of flowers, mature wines of an indefinable mix of spices and oils.

RED WINE GRAPES

■ *Cabernet Sauvignon* is the international star of red grapes: first grown in Bordeaux, it now appears in virtually every wine country. It takes to ageing well, and (like Chardonnay) it is at home with the flavours of oak. It is frequently blended with its cousin Cabernet Franc and/or with Merlot. Cabernets come in all styles, from the young and fruity to the severe, tannic and long-lived. The latter make perhaps the greatest red wines of the world. A scent of ripe berry fruit, a whiff of eucalyptus, a touch of cedar: all are typical Cabernet tasting notes.

■ *Pinot Noir* is the grape of red burgundy, and of many fine red wines in the cooler parts of wine's New World. It is less adaptable than Cabernet, and demands careful culture and winemaking. When properly handled, the result is a wine which when young tastes of strawberries and plums, moves on to smell of violets and climaxes with a rich blend of old leather, ripe fruit and spices.

■ *Syrah* is the least known of the great red grapes, but it shows in the Rhône, with Hermitage and Côte Rôtie, that its wine can be as sublime as any. Australia and California grow it (sometimes as Shiraz) and it adds to the blend of many a southern French wine. Great Syrah takes 20 years to age from black to red, and from tannic ink to subtle luxury, though many other wines mature much faster. Always there is a herby, heady scent and a rich, satisfying taste.

SELFCONSCIOUS STYLES

Winemakers have enormous freedom to choose the style of wine they make. Where they make the wine has a big

Banyuls is a sweet, dark style of wine from southern France: it goes well with foie gras.

influence (see the pages on What Makes a Vineyard) but increasingly, the maker decides on the style.

The first step (after choosing the site for the vineyard) is picking a grape variety. Then come all kinds of choices about the number of grapes you allow the vine to bear, how ripe you pick them, how to make and mature the wine.

Quantity and quality coexist in an uneasy relationship in the maker's mind each time one of these decisions crops up. Nudged by his bank manager, he ought to make as much wine as possible. But the local wine laws (if there are any) and age-old custom whisper in the maker's other ear: the more wine you make, the less good it will be. Modern wine estates can safely make much more wine than in the past, but the rule still applies. So when judging wine styles we need to know what the maker intends. Price tells us a lot, as does the place of origin (as the rest of this book shows). Some winemakers become known for their personal style, rather like musicians or chefs, and the top ones travel the world putting their thumbprint on numerous wines. It is just as valid today to admire the wines of a certain winemaker as to enjoy a given grape or the wines of a favourite region.

WHAT MAKES A VINEYARD?

INSPIRED BY THE VISION of your name on the label, you want to plant a vineyard. Or at least to dream about doing so, with some detail to spice the dream. Where do you choose?

The ideal vineyard site is a sunny hillside, gently sloping, with well-drained soil and a nearby and thirsty town. There will be frost in winter, but not in spring. The sun will shine through the summer, with regular (and nocturnal) rain, but there will be no hailstorms. Nor will there be too much humidity: dry but gentle winds are welcome. The autumn will be lingeringly warm, with a tempest just as the last grapes are harvested (to lower the temperature in the vat-room, and make everyone feel glad to be indoors).

This has been the recipe since the ancient Romans, and probably before. The list of ingredients is long, and the quantities imprecise. In practice, each vineyard has a different mixture and it is this which makes up its personality — and that of the wine it yields.

Today we can make good use of less than ideal sites: the marketplace can be a world away, thanks to container ships. The drainage of the soil can be improved with machines and pipes. There is little we can do to change the climate, though growers find ways to lessen its fiercest effects: planting trees as wind breaks, adopting various ingenious precautions against frost damage.

The further from the ideal, the more work there is to do — and the greater the risk of something going wrong. Failure can mean the loss of an entire year's crop, and hardship for the grower.

HEAT VERSUS SUBTLETY

Note that the ideal is often far from the reality: vines are tough plants, and can and do grow in very varied conditions. A glance at the world map on page 33 shows that they are grown commercially in more than 50 countries, from Africa to north-west Europe.

Where vines are grown shapes the wines they make. A hot climate will yield more, and riper, grapes than a cool one, but some of the best wines are made where the weather is distinctly chilly. Oregon and New Mexico both make wine, but Oregon has the edge in subtle flavour, and so does Western France compared with Morocco. Why? Because with wine grapes, ripeness is by no means all.

The winemaker seeks ripeness allied to acidity, to the right thickness of skin, to the greatest concentration of flavour in juice and flesh. Merely ripe grapes make sweet, strong wine: the more sweetness, the more alcohol, for that is the formula for fermentation. Frequently, hot-country grapes are so sweet that the yeasts which do the fermenting cannot cope. They give up while the wine still contains some natural sugars: the result is a sweet wine.

The cool-country grapes have less sun-given sweetness — they may even need some help, in the form of sweet grape juice or even sugar, if their juice is to ferment properly. But what they lack in sweetness they can make up in flavour, balance, subtlety, finesse — all the things that make wine more than just a drink.

Let's follow the vineyard through the year — and the decades — to see how the checks and balances apply. We will use the seasons of the northern hemisphere: in Australia, New Zealand and South Africa, subtract six months.

PREPARING THE LAND

Assume the land is lying fallow. It must be ploughed; if necessary drained. The great Bordeaux vineyards spend fortunes on drainage pipes, both on laying them and then, decade after decade, in cleaning them out. The owners know that free-draining soil warms up fast in spring and does not stay waterlogged after summer rainstorms. The vine will dive down deep to find the moisture it needs, so a well-drained plot brings another bonus: the deeper-rooted vines are less stressed if the year turns out hot and dry than those which have their roots nearer the surface.

Rich soil is not a requisite. 'The vine must be made to suffer', say the French (who should know). The most inhospitable, stony sites, withering to almost any other crop, suit vines just fine.

Once drained and ploughed to remove weeds, the next step is a trellis to support the vines which, like climbing roses or raspberries, need help to stay up. Some vines are pruned so hard that they form low, compact bushes, but most need

support. The costs of posts and wires is a major part of the bill for a new vineyard. Once the posts are in place, young vines are planted. They will take three years to yield grapes, perhaps four until they can legally make wine.

A vine can live for a century, but its most vigorous period will be between 15–40 years old. Younger vines produce less intensely-flavoured grapes. Really top-class wine estates do not use the wine from young vines, or they demote it to a second, less expensive, wine.

THE VINEYARD CALENDAR

The year's cycle, once the vine is old enough to bear a crop, can be said to begin after the harvest. The autumn winds and the first frosts strip the red-gold leaves from the vines. Frosts help the vine grower, as they do any grower or gardener, by killing pests and the micro-organisms that can cause rot. Some time in winter, pruning takes place. The vineyard workers cut the vines back to a pre-planned shape, allowing a controlled number of buds for next year's growth. Each district has its own tradition of pruning, be it hard or gentle, and different places allow their vines to grow in varying shapes.

Using a horsedrawn plough is gentler to the soil, and more relaxing for the vigneron. This horse, called Reveuse ('Dreamer') works at Château Magdelaine in St-Emilion.

Some are man-high, with many fruiting branches or canes, and a basketful of fruit; others are but waist-height with just two branches and a few handfuls of bunches per vine.

It is bitterly cold as the smoke of the burning vine prunings drifts through the bleak winter vineyards, but by early spring there are signs of life on the stark, bare vines. Buds thicken, and with the growing warmth they sprout green shoots — just in time, in bad-luck years, for frost to kill them. Growers light stoves among the vines, or blow air with giant wind-mills, to counter frost. The best defence is a sloping site: cold air drains away downhill.

Traditional growers plough the soil between the vines in spring. This lets air into the roots, discourages weeds and dis-turbs the habitats of dormant pests. Other growers reckon that ploughing is old hat: the weight of the tractor damages the soil, and studies have shown that unploughed land both soaks up rain, and survives frost, better than ploughed.

In June the vines, now in full leaf, flower. The flowers are

Old vines in early spring: the seemingly dead stump has been pruned back hard over the winter, but the dormant buds are about to break out into green shoots.

for warm, dry weather. Rain now will swell the grapes, diluting their flavour, and may lead to rot in the close-packed bunches.

Once the grapes are ripe enough, speed is vital to pick them before they grow over-ripe, or before autumn rain can ruin them. You sometimes hear wine growers discussing the success or failure of a vintage. Some estate or château may be said to have 'picked before the rain': they took the decision to pick when the grapes were not quite as ready as they would hope, but before the weather broke. Neighbours who waited for an extra degree of ripeness may have lost the gamble and struggled to get in a harvest of sodden, rot-infected fruit.

DECISIONS, DECISIONS...

There is a story about a modern French businessman who wanted to get away from the pressures and decisions of the office, so he gave it all up and bought a farm. Within a couple of years he was back at a desk, surrounded by papers and telephones — but with a bustling farm outside the window. Wine growing, unfortunately, means more decisions and choices than most sorts of agriculture.

At every stage there are choices. To prune hard, or little. To plough and to spray, or not. To pick now or later. Perfectionists will thin out their grapes in the summer (a 'green harvest') to lessen an over-large crop, reasoning that too many grapes will mean dilute-tasting wine.

And the weather is acting in concert with these choices. To say that winemaking is predictable is to ignore both the effect of all these decisions, and the weather's bearing on the grower's labours.

It is hardly surprising that the end of picking has traditionally been the occasion for an epic party. It is hard, back-breaking work, as like as not carried out in frantic shifts in the face of some impending storm. At last the grapes are safely in the winery, and the camaraderie and sense of achievement is enormous.

And now, there is just the matter of making the wine....

not a spectacular sight: mere clusters of greenish white, hardly visible against the leaves. The weather is critical: a warm flowering means a large crop, as the flowers set into immature bunches of grapes. A cool wet flowering sets the vine back and it can rarely recover. Growers know that the flowering decides the size, and a lot of the quality, of the year's crop.

Summer means spraying against pests such as red spider and various caterpillars, and diseases such as rot and mildew. The vine canes are tied to the trellis or posts, wayward tendrils are trimmed back. Much debate takes place about how much summer pruning a vine should get: green growth shields the grapes from scorching (useful in hot climates) but can impede ripening in cool ones.

As August moves into September, the grapes swell and change colour: greeny-gold or red-purple. The grower starts to check their ripeness. Taste will tell a lot, but instruments to measure sugar and acidity are now common. Everyone hopes

MAKING WINE

As MANY AMATEURS have proved, making wine demands nothing more technical than a bath-tub. Italian communities, cut off from their homeland's abundant wine in cold London or New York, have traditionally made garage wines from grapes bought by the box in the wholesale fruit market. A bath-tub or similar vessel holds the grapes, a plunger (or the traditional feet) is used to crush them and the pulpy mass starts spontaneously to ferment.

Prohibition drove California grape growers, deprived of their winery customers, to sell jars of grape juice to city-dwellers labelled with the warning 'do not add yeasts or the contents will ferment'. Alas for temperance, few buyers seem to have read the label.

What is fermentation? The reaction between certain micro-organisms, called yeasts, which live on the outside of the grape skins, and sugar, which is found within in the form of fructose and glucose in ripe grape-juice. The reaction produces heat, alcohol, carbon dioxide gas and many minor chemicals, some of which contribute to the flavour of the resulting wine. The fermentation goes on, bubbling and frothing, for as long as the yeast spores find sugar to feed on. When all the sugar has been used up, the yeasts die. Sometimes the process is self-regulating: so much heat is produced that the yeasts are stunned and stop work.

The end result is wine. Very new wine, still in need of separating from the grape skins, pips and stalks, but wine.

Everything the winemaker does is a refinement on a process, that of fermentation, which is entirely natural. By the use of heat and cold, the winemaker can start and stop fermentation, and to an extent control it; but the goings-on inside the vat are the business of the yeasts, not the maker. Some wineries import special strains of yeast, others let those on the grape skins have their head.

So anyone can make wine of sorts. But making wine of quality and individuality is another matter. It depends first on having good grapes: if they do not have much flavour, or are under- or over-ripe, there is not much the winemaker can do.

Workers in a Bordeaux cellar top up each cask to make sure there is no air space, which could lead to wine spoiling.

Given good fruit, the winemaker can attempt to steer nature towards something sublime.

Temperature is the winemaker's tool. Modern wineries have vats which can be heated or cooled, allowing fermentation to be kept going slowly, if that is desired, and to stop the fermentation getting too hot. In former times — which means about 20 years ago — wineries had to tip blocks of ice into the vats to cool things down. Or, if the weather was cold, fires would be lit in the vat-house to start the fermentation off. As a last resort, bodily warmth, in the person of the workforce, would be used to warm the juice up.

PRESSING AND CRUSHING

Before fermentation, the grapes have to be crushed to allow their juice to run free. This used to be done by treading. It still is, in a few places. Human feet are gentle and cheap, and not as unhygienic as many think: the alcohol acts as a

disinfectant. Today a wide range of types of press are used. Red grapes are crushed, not pressed. The difference is important: for red wine, only gentle crushing is needed as the skins and juice can go into the fermenting-vat together. The pulp and juice of even a black grape is clear, so the skins are needed to add colour, as well as flavours, to the wine. If white wine is the aim, then the grapes are both crushed and pressed, usually in the same machine. The pressing forces the juice out, leaving the skins and pips behind. Even green grapes contribute colour to the wine: some 'skin contact' is reckoned a good idea by modern white-wine makers, who welcome the extra flavour the skins confer. But the juice is always filtered to remove them before fermentation begins.

Once the fermentation is over, the rest is a process of care, judgement and time. Care comes in the form of the removal of yeast particles and other solids which make the wine look cloudy. The modern methods used for this are centrifuges and filters. Critics say these can strip wines of flavour as well as cloudiness. Chilling can be used to help force particles to fall to the bottom of the storage tank or vat: this is a modern version of the process which took place naturally in winter in old-fashioned wineries.

Red wines are not routinely filtered — at least quality wines are not (everyday wine made on an industrial scale uses every technique to ease the flow of predictable, sterile wine). Fining and racking achieve the same effect: the new wine is put into casks and then allowed to rest. Solid particles in the wine naturally fall to the bottom, and they are helped along by fining. This involves adding substances such as beaten egg white which are coagulants: they attract particles floating in the wine and carry them to the bottom.

After a time the wine is pumped or poured into a new cask, carefully leaving the residue behind. This is racking. A young

A Chianti cellar: the Riecine estate makes fine Chianti Classico which is aged in large casks like those in the background.

red wine, ageing for up to two and a half years in oak casks, may be racked several times before bottling.

MATURING THE WINE

The idea that wine gets better if kept was known to the Romans, who sealed clay wine jars (*amphorae*) with pitch and cork. It was rediscovered in the 17th and 18th centuries, when the ageing of wine in casks became normal in Bordeaux, Germany, Italy and elsewhere. This demanded not just well-made and well-maintained casks, but also the systematic application of techniques like fining and racking and topping-up casks to replace wine lost by evaporation.

Winemakers used casks to hold and mature wine because that was all they had. Vats of concrete, steel and plastic became available only in the 20th century. The shape and size of the casks was determined by pragmatism: the *barrique*, a cask of 225 litres common for storage in France, was and is the right size for two men to move around in a cellar. It also (by accident?) is exactly the right size and shape to allow the wine to come into contact with the wood of the cask. A smaller cask means more wood to wine: a larger, less.

Much mystique attends the use of casks for ageing wine. Bordeaux châteaux, and those wineries in the New World which have copied them, use a proportion of new oak barrels. The idea is that the new wood adds welcome flavours to the wine. These include oak tannins (as distinct from the tannins in grape skins), phenols including vanillin, and many others.

The winemaker must make many choices about ageing. How long, for a start, should the wine spend in cask or vat before bottling and sale? Some places have wine laws which lay down a minimum time: a Spanish *gran reserva* wine must have had at least two years in cask, and three in bottle, before sale. Normally it is up to the winemaker, who may feel that some years need more time than others. A vintage when the wine is light demands less time in cask, for the lighter wine risks being overwhelmed by the wood's tastes.

The next choice is how many, if any, of the casks should be new. Only a powerful, richly-flavoured wine can cope with new oak. Only the very best wines can manage 100% new oak — and justify the very considerable expense. Most winemakers would allow only a percentage of new oak. Another option is to buy once-used barrels from a property which does use new oak each year.

Winemakers can get excited about who makes the barrels, and which forest the oak comes from. This is not as mad as it seems, for oaks have different structures: some allow the wine to breathe more than others, some confer their flavour compounds more readily than others.

INTO THE BOTTLE

At some point — in weeks for a white wine to be drunk fresh and young, after years for a grand red — the wine is bottled. It is usual to mix the contents of the various storage vats to achieve a consistent wine, as vats and barrels will vary. Some regions, such as parts of Germany, traditionally bottle the wines a cask at a time, but this is now an expensive luxury.

Bottles must be sterile, also corks; and the corks must be chosen with care. The bottling line, a clanking monster, may be at the château or at a merchant's premises. Some areas even have mobile bottling lines built into trucks.

The final act is to apply a label and box the new bottles in cartons for shipment. Some wineries, especially those making quality and sparkling wines, give the bottled wine a period of further ageing to let it rest and settle.

This, like buying new oak casks each year, is an expensive option: the winemaker needs the space to store the wine — and, of course, the longer it is stored the longer before someone pays for it. The expense, and passion, that goes into creating great wine is a world away from the more industrial making of the basic, everyday drink — and each winemaker has only so many vintages in a lifetime to make the attempt.

WINE & FOOD

SOME WINES ARE INTENDED to be drunk on their own, but most are made with food in mind. They belong at meal-times. Many newcomers to wine want to know exactly which wine goes with which kind of food. There are some answers, but no rules. It is more helpful to think of wines and *occasions*. Conjure up in your mind the atmosphere of the meal: is it a picnic or a banquet? Do the people sharing the meal care about wine, or is it, to them, just another detail: helping the occasion along, but not there to be thought about?

It soon becomes clear that there are straightforward, summer-afternoon wines and ultra-sophisticated, complex, special-occasion wines — with many halts on the line in between. Choose the right kind of wine and you are more than halfway there.

LISTS ARE NOT LAW

When it comes to detailed guidance on just which bottle goes with a certain dish, the answers will differ with the person you ask — and where you ask the question, too. Many of the original lists of 'rules' have a strong French slant, because that's where people first started to take gastronomy seriously. Recent efforts have come largely from California, which is where people seem most to like making up score-cards and lists. Try to follow the advice in Sydney or Singapore or Scotland, however, and things will start to go wrong. Even the classic dishes which are found on restaurant menus worldwide will change in many subtle ways depending on where they are being created. The world's food stores increasingly sell ingredients from around the globe, but a Cape Town restaurant's repertoire will, inevitably, be different from that of a Stockholm one.

There have been attempts to compile lists of perfect partnerships, based upon elaborate tasting and sampling. But repeat the experiments, and you will soon find the snags. Your way of cooking, say, a simple roast chicken will not be the same as mine: most cooks use an almost instinctive battery of flavourings and condiments of their own: a little salt and pepper, some butter or oil.... Heavily herbed? Stuffed with sage and onion? Or with lemon and butter? Laden with garlic? Then the accompanying vegetables, sauces, gravy.... It's clear

that to choose a wine because a wine and food pundit says it goes with roast chicken is aiming at a very broad target.

So take such lists as guidelines and suggestions, not decrees. After all, if a red Bordeaux is recommended, which one? There are several thousand. And which vintage? If the advice *is* specific, you turn to your wine rack and find that you do not happen to have a bottle of Château Lanessan 1991. If the advice is general you are faced with the wide variation in taste and style among all those clarets.

So there are no outright rules. Which is a good thing. No-one drinks wine to follow rules and regulations. It's supposed to be fun. Look instead, if in doubt or need of inspiration, for starting-points:

MATCHING HOMELANDS

The easiest way to partner wine and food with success is to begin with what is local. If the food is modern Californian, try California wines. If the restaurant is seriously Provençal, stick to the wines of southern France. Not all restaurants, or cookbooks, or chefs, are authentic, but the starting point is there. Regional cuisines have spent generations instinctively matching food and wine. It is perhaps too perfect to think that the wines evolved to match the local food, as the wine-makers have to contend with climate, soil and a few other factors too. But there often is a synergy.

Travel in central Spain and you will find marvellous roast lamb, baked in the oven and served very simply. It goes well with the red wines of the Ribero del Duero and Rioja districts: they are usually drunk when quite mature, with their harsh edges softened but with a certain amount of oaky tannin and acidity. Perfect partners to the succulent lamb. Cross the Pyrenees and around Toulouse, in southern France, they have a passion for goose and duck, often cooking these rich-tasting birds in ways that make them richer and more pungent still. No-one offers you a rich, heady wine. The local vineyards supply light but tasty reds such as Frontonnais, Gaillac, Buzet to balance the meal.

This trick does not always work, usually because some regional cuisines put the food, very firmly, first. This is true of much traditional German cooking, which does not really suit the local wines (or at least the wines the locals make now). Germans, and many Italians, find that the time to drink their best local wines is before or after the meal. In Germany that means carafe wines (often delicious) or beer at meal-time; in Italy ditto, but the beer is less good.

MATCHING STYLE

The pages on choosing wine (pages 10-11) explain how wines can vary: dry to sweet, light to heavy. These are the first clue to what goes with what. It is usually a mistake to partner a strong-tasting, assertive dish with a similar wine. A rich, oily fish does not need an oaky, unctuous New World Chardonnay, it demands a crisp acidic wine. It can even be a red....The logic works both ways. Say you have a lovely bottle of mature Bordeaux or Cabernet Sauvignon. Do not plan a meal with a very rich, or spicy, main course: it will dominate, even kill, the fine flavours of the wine. Roast some lamb, or a chicken, and let the wine stand out. Good,

mature, wines deserve priority over the food: there are after all not *that* many really good bottles in anyone's collection.

PLANNING A MEAL

Another fault of the didactic 'this goes with that' approach is to fail to consider the meal as a whole. If it is just family supper, then one wine can be picked to complement the main (or, indeed, only) dish. But if there are friends coming round, or perhaps a grander occasion altogether, meriting the term 'dinner party', then there are more choices to be made. What do you drink before the meal? If there are two or more courses, should there be a wine with each? And what about afterwards? The whole thing can get out of hand, with too many wines for the bemused guests to cope

No problems about food and wine matching at the Paulée de Meursault, the enormous bring-your-own party which the growers of Meursault hold each November. Everyone brings their best wines, which they share with their table companions. The food is all predictably Burgundian.

with. Some occasions are really built around the wines: like-minded people get together to appraise and enjoy fine wines and the meal is just the setting. Most of us like to balance the food and the wine, with a good added sprinkling of conversation and fun.

Where and when you eat matters, too. A wine which tastes good in a cold climate, or in winter, may not show so well on a hot summer night or in the tropics — even if the host has taken care to serve it at the right temperature. There are summer wines, too: many a disappointment comes from taking those wonderful holiday wines home. It used to be said that they 'did not travel'. Perhaps summer pool-side wines just do not taste good back in a rainy northern-hemisphere November. Lunchtime wines should be lighter, simpler, than dinner wines — unless the luncheon is a very grand affair, and no-one is expected to do any work after it.

THROUGH THE MEAL

Before you eat, something refreshing and appetising is called for. Champagne has almost a monopoly here — or rather sparkling wine has. Those bubbles do stimulate appetite, wit and talk. Some sparkling wines, particularly from the New World, are really a little too sweet for pre-dinner drinking. They are made with general social occasions in mind, and suit them very well. If the meal is important, try out a bottle beforehand, looking for a gentle 'cut' of acidity as well as enough fruit to allow the wine to be enjoyed without food.

The same advice goes for still white wine served before a meal. Still or sparkling, white wine should be really well-cooled. It will warm up fast in the glasses in a warm room.

Whites served before the meal should not be too dry or too heavy: a Mosel, an unoaked Chardonnay, a Loire wine.

The order in which wines are served at table depends on the food. But there are some useful principles which apply to wines themselves: work up from the simpler to the better, from younger to older, from white to red, from dry to sweet.

SOME PAIRINGS TO AVOID

Wine was originally part of a specific diet, that of the Mediterranean and Europe. Serve it with food from a totally different culture and it may not work so well. There are wines

Wine, cheese and grapes: a perfect, and perfectly simple, meal.

that fit Indonesian, or Mexican, or Finnish, food. But more often than not such cuisines work better with the drink that their culture developed alongside the food — or with cold beer or fruit drinks.

The gentler forms of Indian and Chinese/South-East Asian cooking can partner wine well. The first rule is to serve nothing too subtle: keep your old and best bottles for plainer food. Experiments show that vintage champagne goes rather well with Chinese, especially Peking, food — until you get the bill. Cold sparkling wine from less exalted places does almost as well. Very cold white wines, across the spectrum from bone dry to medium sweet, taste good with Chinese dishes. Anything really dry is apt to clash with the often slightly sweet flavours in the food, so go for a wine with a bit of body, such as New World Chardonnay or Riesling. Soft, clear-flavoured red wines do well with Chinese food, and with the more lightly-spiced Indian curries.

Vinegar, often used in salad dressings, does nothing at all for the taste of wine. If a dressing is needed, use white or red wine, or lemon juice, in it instead.

Artichokes famously make wine taste odd, as does chocolate — though some enjoy the experience. Eggs, in the form of soufflés and omelettes, seem to deaden the taste of wine, which makes such dishes worth avoiding if the wines matter.

SOME RULES TO BE BROKEN

■ *White wine with fish, red with meat* is a good generalisation. Some fish works well with light red wines drunk cool. Salmon, tuna, herrings, mackerel — all oily fish — work well with reds. More subtle fish, such as plaice and sole, asks for a crisp white wine.

Red wine with red meat is usually a good idea, but pork and poultry are good with solid, well-flavoured whites like a Graves, Alsace or white Rioja. Cold meat, too, is enjoyable with white wine. Sometimes what goes with the meat matters more than the meat itself: strong sauces make more demands on the wine.

■ *Red wine goes with cheese*: this one deserves more scepticism. The French habit of serving cheese before dessert, so foreign to the Anglo-Saxons who swap the order round, allows the last of the main-course red to be finished with the cheese. Choose the cheese well, and this is fine. They should be mild, unassertive hard cheeses: mature Dutch Gouda, moderately pungent

English cheeses such as Wensleydale or Cheshire. Soft cheeses are possible when young, but when they have reached the really ripe stage they will kill any red wine, especially a fine old one. Try dry or medium white wines with soft cheese, especially goat's cheese. Really strong, salty cheeses such as Roquefort have been known to work with Sauternes and other sweet wines. The English tradition is to drink port with cheese, right at the end of the meal, and this can work well. Provide some nuts, such as walnuts and brazils, and perhaps a few ripe figs, and the combination is even better.

■ *Sweet wine goes with pudding*: the modern shibboleth of the 'pudding wine' ruins a lot of lovely bottles. Sauternes and other late-harvest wines, especially German ausleses and so on, are too subtle for heavy, creamy puddings. But hosts seem to think no dinner party is complete without at least three puddings and a bottle of something sticky. The best wines with such puddings are sweet Muscats and fortified wines: southern France has plenty, California and Australia also make them. An Austrian sweet wine will work better than the more delicate Germans. The fine sweet wines thus displaced should be served with a few ripe peaches, or on their own. The adventurous partner them with ripe soft cheeses.

SOME WINES TO TRY

A list is a lot more use than all these generalisations. The caveats made above preclude many more specifics — they really do restrict rather than help — but there are some wines which people forget in their menu planning. After, or perhaps before, thinking about the ubiquitous Chardonnays and Cabernets, try the following.

■ *Sparkling wine* works very well with many first courses, and you can start a bottle before the meal and take it on to the table. Aside from champagne, look for terms like 'bottle-fermented' on the label, replacing '*méthode champenoise*', now no longer allowed.

■ *Sherry* — and its imitators — is a great food wine. Dry sorts such as fino and manzanilla are light enough to go well with food, and have a special affinity with smoked fish, a food hard to match with other wines.

■ *Riesling whites,* if made to be dry (or allowed to mature towards dryness) have the acidity, body and character to partner quite assertive foods. And they make a refreshing change from Chardonnay.

■ *Pinot Grigio*, or *Pinot Gris*, is an excellent food white: it has body with dryness.

■ *Merlot reds* offer a sweetness and softness not often found in 'serious' Cabernets. The Merlot flavour works well with the sweeter, richer meat dishes such as beef casseroles.

■ *Italian reds* can go with more than pasta. They have an astringency and slight bitterness that makes them welcome when the dish is unctuous and rich. They also work well with vegetable dishes.

■ *Loire whites* from the sweeter end of the spectrum, such as Vouvray, are delicious alone and with a wide range of foods, though not rich puddings.

■ *Port*, especially aged tawny, is good chilled as an unusual apéritif, and it goes well with cheese and some rich, pastry-based desserts.

■ *Sherries* such as old Oloroso, which is dry, or sweet Olorosos and 'old-landed' sherries, are fine alternatives to port at the end of a meal.

TRY IT, IT WON'T KILL YOU

Why not experiment? There is great pleasure to be had from opening two or more wines and trying them out with the dishes on the table. If something tastes odd, stop drinking it. Put the cork back in and keep it until tomorrow. The only time a food and wine combination can go badly wrong is in a restaurant, where inappropriate matches cost money as well as pleasure. Ask for advice from proprietor or waiter: if an air of uncertainty attends the answer, stick to the house wine.

A special party at home can go wrong if the wine does not fit, but the answer is to try it out beforehand. If possible, try the whole menu out, not necessarily with the wines you plan to serve, but with something of similar character. Then on the day (or night) itself you can relax rather than worry — about the wine, at least.

STARTING A CELLAR

A CELLAR IS NOT NECESSARILY a hole in the ground. It is, in wine terms, something much more interesting: a store or hoard of bottles. It can be kept in a corner of your house or apartment, in a wine merchant's warehouse, or even beneath the garden. Starting a cellar does not mean grabbing a spade, it implies acquiring more wine than you intend to drink tonight, or over the next week. Get a month ahead of likely consumption, and you have started a cellar.

A cellar is also a collection. It is a stock of bottles gathered with some thought, with the idea of (at the very least) avoiding the danger of running out of wine. It will, ideally, be more than that: a cellar can ensure that you have the right wine, in the best possible condition, and at the keenest price.

Wine collecting has gained a bad name, due to the antics of some who buy wine more to look at than to drink. If the lure of keeping and hoarding old bottles catches you, make them a part rather than the whole of your collection.

If a bottle that indisputably belonged to that wine-loving American president Thomas Jefferson (who sought out France's best on the spot in the 1780s) comes up for sale, it would plainly rank as an antique rather than a drink. But otherwise, wine is, for sure, made to be drunk and the point of collecting it is to have enough of the right wines to drink, when you need them.

Beware, likewise, of buying purely for investment. More 'investors' have lost than gained: no-one can be sure how a wine is going to age; vintages rise and fall in relative reputation, and thus value. The 1982 and 1983 red Bordeaux vintages cost about the same when new: a decade later the '82s were twice the price of the '83s. Few wines have 'earned' enough to cover the loss, due to inflation and foregone interest, in having their purchase price tied up for a decade. The only good reason to buy wine early in its life is to ensure you

May your cellar be this well stocked: bottles of fine Bordeaux rest in serried ranks.

have the wines you want: mature fine wines are hard to buy.

As wine shops get better, and even the neighbourhood food store in many places sells tolerable wine, the need to hoard or collect does diminish. It was, not that long ago, the only way to ensure a supply of reliable wine. Before the days of wine stores, people (usually quite prosperous people) would buy a cask of wine and the wine merchant would send a man along to help bottle it. Grand houses had their own bottles, with the owner's crest embossed in the glass.

The hangover from these days permeates the vocabulary of cellars and wine collection. All the talk about laying down, and bins, comes from a century ago. The old wine drinkers would have far fewer kinds of wine than us, but many more bottles of the same kind. A barrel of claret or port would last even the most thirsty Victorian household quite a long time, and one wonders if they got bored with always drinking the same wine. At least they could study its maturity curve.

The Victorian cellar (always below ground: architects knew what was expected of them) would have no single-bottle racks of the kind we buy in hardware store. It would have bins: brick or stone alcoves in which the bottles would be piled (or 'laid down'). A bin would hold a cask's-worth of bottles. The surviving habit of 'bin numbers' on restaurant wine lists dates from this period.

The point about cellaring is not just getting the right wine, but treating it properly when you have got it. The Victorian bin was ideal: the wine slept horizontally, in a dark, cool place where the temperature changed little and the humidity was quite high. As sale prices of ancient bottles from such cellars prove, nowhere, except perhaps the cellar beneath the château where the wine was made, provides better storage conditions.

CELLAR CONDITIONS

The most important thing is to ensure a steady temperature. It can be quite high, or quite low, but it must be steady. Wine gets better over time because a complex chemical reaction is going on inside the bottle. This process is temperature-sensitive. In warm conditions it happens faster — and the wine matures more quickly. But if the temperature rises and falls rapidly, this seems to stress the process and damages the wine. A temperature above 20°C (68°F) is too warm; below 5°C (41°F) too cold. Freezing ruins wine by forcing out the corks, because freezing liquids expand.

Cellars need fresh air, paradoxically enough. If the air is stagnant, then mould and rot may set in, ruining your corks as well as your house timbers. There should be air vents, perhaps ones that can be closed when very cold or very warm.

A cellar should not be *too* damp, for damp ruins wine labels (they float off) and can encourage rot. Nor should it be *too* dry, for that can cause corks to contract, which will lead to spoilage. Perfection is a relative humidity of 75%.

Finally, a cellar should be dark. Light causes whites to fade in taste, and it is especially damaging to sparkling wines.

CREATING THE IDEAL CELLAR

Lacking, as most of us do, a 19th-century or earlier cellar, we have to try to replicate the ideal conditions elsewhere. The only way to ensure an even temperature is to insulate. This is what an underground cellar offers: a few feet of rock or stone or earth to insulate the contents from the changing conditions outside. (Modern insulation materials can replace rock walls, but the insulation needs to be there.)

Most houses and apartments have cool corners and warm ones. To search out the wine-friendly corners eliminate the hot-spots first: near the heating boiler, close to hot pipes, the kitchen — however decorative wine racks look. Pipes can be lagged or insulated, but it is hard to completely cover them. And all kitchens go through extremes of heat and humidity. Look for the cupboards and alcoves on the cool side of the house, away from the sun. Fruitful areas to explore are under the stairs, in basements, and in cupboards in little-used rooms. Buy a maximum-minimum thermometer and try the temperature in the likely places.

Outbuildings such as garages are possible sites, but they can experience extremes of heat and cold. You will need to check the temperature over a longer period, and work harder at the insulation.

If there is really no suitable corner, and you want to keep wine over a long period, you might consider a purpose-made wine cabinet. These are like refrigerators, but with a heating element too and a sensitive thermostat. They keep wine at a set temperature, and the best ones also have ventilation to ensure a gentle air circulation.

A more ambitious solution is to dig a cellar. This can be less of an adventure if a modular cellar is bought. These are sunk in to a hole beneath the house, or the garage, and lined with concrete units which both form the walls and provide storage bins for your bottles.

ORGANISING YOUR CELLAR

The first need is a system of shelves or racks so wines can be stored on their sides. This can be as simple as wooden shelves, divided by regular uprights, and of a size to hold a dozen bottles on their sides: the corks must stay damp. Or it can be a complex of racks for single bottles. Most cellars need both: racks for odd bottles and mini-bins for wine bought by the half-dozen, dozen or (if you are lucky) larger amounts.

Make sure the shelves and racks are well secured to the wall: wine is heavy. Racks can be bought in kit form, in standard sizes, or tailor-made to fit a particular alcove.

If space allows, provide a small table or shelf for decanting, writing notes and general clutter. There should be a good light, but not an automatic light switch (like a refrigerator) as these can stick on and can raise the temperature.

WHICH WINES TO KEEP?

Not all wines improve with keeping, however perfect the conditions. Most white wines are made to be drunk young, as indeed are most reds. There is a clear distinction between reds made with ageing in mind and those which are aimed at the less patient. Sometimes you will find a wine which though humble in price and origin has the 'backbone' for keeping. The section on tasting explains how to spot such wines.

Red wines to cellar include many made from Cabernet Sauvignon, such as Bordeaux and the various 'New World' Cabernets. Syrah or Shiraz wines can also age well: examples are Rhône reds from France, Australian Shiraz. Some Italian wines, such as Barolo, are made to age. Many New World reds promise much with their deep colour and ripe fruit, but not all are designed for keeping. Look for the tannin and structure ('carpentry', as the French say) behind the fruit.

White wines to keep are essentially good Rieslings, the best Chardonnays (burgundies particularly) and some oddities like Australian Sémillon.

Fortified wines such as vintage port are made to mature for decades, and are undrinkable until they have done so. Good champagne gets better with bottle age, especially vintage champagne, but do not age ordinary sparkling wines, which are nearly all made to be drunk when fresh.

The wine cellar at a great hotel points towards perfection: solid, well-built and well-filled racks.

KEEPING RECORDS

Once you have a cellar full of wine, be it a corner of a cupboard or a vaulted chamber, the next problem is remembering what you have got, and when it will be ready.

It can be difficult to keep track of when wines are bought, how long they ought to be kept, and when they should be at their peak. Try to keep a notebook listing when you got the wines (and for how much), and perhaps when drunk. No-one can be sure when a wine is 'ready': try it, if you have several bottles of the same wine. Wine magazines offer plenty of (sometimes conflicting) advice. If in doubt, open wines early rather than late in their life-span: a young wine will open up in decanter or glass, whereas once too old, a wine is but a shadow of its perfect state.

Few wines need keeping for decades: broadly, the only bottles than need more than ten years are great red Bordeaux, vintage port, and great sweet whites such as Sauternes and Rhine wines. Comments on ageing wines are to be found in the chapters on regions and countries.

TRICKS OF THE TRADE

THE PLEASURES OF WINE are there for the enjoying, given the most basic equipment: a glass and a corkscrew. A little care, most of it expended in forethought, can make wine even more enjoyable. This care is best applied in getting the temperature right, while the choice of glasses, even of corkscrews, can add a lot to the occasion.

SERVING WINE

Get the white wine cool and not much else matters. That is the trick of successful wine serving in a sentence. Ignore advice to warm red wine: it was worth doing when the average home had a cellar where the thermometer read at Arctic levels, and the dining room was not a lot warmer. Today we live in more comfort, and there is more chance of red wine being too warm than too cold.

White wine, and sparkling wine, tastes best when it is between 6–12°C (43–54°F). Whites are most enjoyable cool because, when warm, their acidity grows more noticeable. We

enjoy acidity in white wine: a brisk 'cut' is part of their character. But allow the wine to warm, and the acidity gets out of balance: the taste becomes flabby. A cool wine blends acidity with fruit into an appetising whole.

The simpler the wine, the cooler it should be served. Fine white wines, particularly sweet ones, need to be at the warmer end of the above scale. And although sparkling wines should be served cool, fine vintage champagnes also deserve to be a little warmer.

A red wine served too cold will not give of its best — though it may taste refreshing. Warmth allows the flavour compounds in the wine to emerge as scents. Keep the wine cool, and they stay locked up. This is also the reason for serving good white wines a little warmer than simple ones: there is no point in drinking a fine, complex wine so cold it tastes of little or nothing.

Simple, young red wines are enjoyable lightly chilled: try around 12–15°C (54–60°F). Older, finer wines are at their best around 16–18°C (61–65°F). No wine should be served warmer than this.

You can, if you want, buy thermometers to check temperature: either the sort that clip onto the outside of a bottle, or ones that drop into the neck once the cork is pulled. If serving wine at a long meal, such as a dinner party, expect the temperature in the room to rise during the meal: peoples' body heat, and candles, combine to raise the mercury quite a bit. It may be worth keeping the red wines in another room (but not the equally overheated kitchen) until they are served.

Outdoor events in summer make it very hard to keep white wine cold and to stop red wine warming past the point of enjoyment. Do not hesitate to use an ice bucket on red wines, and make sure there is plenty of ice in reserve.

COOLING WINE DOWN

The domestic refrigerator will chill wine from room temperature down to white-wine serving level in about two hours. If,

Fine old wines demand decanting, and this elegant engine helps: turn the handle and the bottle gently tilts, allowing the wine to flow into the decanter.

that is, the refrigerator is not packed full of food, and not constantly opened and shut in a warm room. In such circumstances the chilling process can take four hours.

An ice bucket is a surer — and much quicker — way to chill wine. Get a big bucket, ideally one that holds two bottles with enough room around them for plenty of ice and water, and which is tall enough to chill the wine up to the neck.

The common mistake is to use too much ice. A mixture of ice and water is, paradoxically, more efficient. The water allows the heat to be conducted away from the bottle: ice alone will not do this. The ice-and-water mix will cool a bottle from room to serving temperature in about 15 minutes.

All wines are best stored cool, like any food. The best way to have cool wine is to move to a house with a cool cellar (such a drastic solution may make the modern alternative, a chilled cabinet, seem reasonable). Failing that, just store bottles on their side in as cool and dark a corner that you can find (*see* page 24), and allow time for further chilling as necessary. Ignore fitted-kitchen manufacturers who attempt to build in wine racks next to the stove. Do not keep wine for very long periods in an ordinary refrigerator: it dulls the taste, and can even lead to the transfer of smells from foods to wine.

OPENING THE BOTTLE

Between you and the wine are a cork and a capsule: the plastic, foil or wax cover over the top of the cork and the neck of the bottle. Why are corks still used? They seem old-fashioned and organic in a world of convenience and speed, but they are tremendously efficient seals. Cork is very elastic: force it into the bottle-neck (special machines are used) and it will spring back to fill the neck with an excellent seal. Cork is durable, and will not be affected by, or affect, the wine. Only the (very) occasional insect can bore through the cork.

Corks fall down when they are not sterilised properly. In these conditions, moulds and spores can find their way into the cork and affect the wine. A wine hit by this will be ruined: sour, dead and stinking. This is the origin of the term 'corked'. It has nothing to do with the bits of cork left floating in the glass by inefficient corkscrews. Have a sniff at a corked wine if you come across one: it is unmistakable once smelled.

The best way to remove the capsule is with a small knife. Some corkscrews, the 'waiter's friend' sort, have a knife built into the handle like a penknife. Some capsules have a little tag to pull. We all end up picking at the edges with a finger, and we can all expect to be cut by sharp edges of foil. I was once cut twice in a month by the same wine, whose maker had discovered a particularly vicious metal capsule.

Take the capsule off, or cut the top off cleanly. Do not let the wine touch the capsule when poured, for fear of tainting it. Wipe the rim of the bottle with a clean cloth.

CORKSCREWS

Invest in a good corkscrew: it will save many frustrating struggles and a few ruined bottles. The needs are few, but rarely met. The screw must be wide, and shaped as an open spiral, not a solid shaft. It should look like a worm, not a drill-bit. This is because an open spiral grips the cork, while a solid shaft bores through it. There is little more annoying than a corkscrew which carefully drills a hole through the cork — and then pulls out not the cork but a shower of fragments.

The other point about a corkscrew is leverage. You need a strong arm to pull a cork out unaided by some mechanical advantage. Rather than a straightforward T-shaped corkscrew, choose a model where the spiral pushes against the neck of the bottle, or with a lever action.

OPENING SPARKLING WINE

Fizzy wine will go everywhere if it is not opened properly, a trait motor racing stars exploit at the expense of their sponsors. If you want to drink your champagne, not bathe in it, get the wine cold before you try to open it. Warm wine is fizzier: the warmth causes more and bigger bubbles to appear, and the pressure grows greater. Do not shake the bottle, for the same reason.

Take your chilled bottle, stand it upright, not beneath a priceless chandelier, and carefully remove the foil. Underneath will be found the cork, held in place by a little 'cage' of wire. This will be secured by a twisted loop of wire at one side. Place a thumb over the top of the cork, and with the other hand slowly untwist the loop. The plan is to carefully remove the cage while keeping a tight hold of the cork.

Grasp the cork with one hand, and the base of the bottle with the other. Point the bottle away from people, windows, mirrors (or that chandelier). Slowly and gently turn the *bottle*, not the cork. This applies greater leverage. You will feel the cork start to move. Hold on tight, and you can ease it out with a gentle 'pop' — and no wasted wine. Have a glass standing by, just in case.

DECANTING

More fuss is made about decanting than anything else to do with wine. It is perfectly possible to go through a lifetime of wine enjoyment without resorting to decanting. The point of it is to separate a wine from the solid deposit that builds up in some bottles. Nine wines in ten never develop any deposit, and even fine red wines only do so when they are quite old. If you do not drink such wines, then the problem will not arise.

There is another reason for decanting, though: to aerate a young wine and allow it to open up and develop more taste due to the action of the air. This kind of decanting is merely opening and pouring: no special technique is needed, except a clean jug or decanter.

If you find a wine with a deposit — and the way to tell is to hold the bottle up to the light, after it has been lying down, and look for the black sludge — then the worst part of decanting can still be avoided. Just stand the bottle up for two or three days. The deposit will fall to the bottom of the bottle. Then, taking care not to disturb the deposit, open the bottle as normal and pour the wine in a gentle stream into a decanter, leaving the sludge in the bottle. A steady hand, and a funnel, should avoid any getting into the decanter.

Decanting gets tricky only if the bottle is taken straight from horizontal storage to the decanter. Use a cradle or basket to move the wine, keeping it horizontal to avoid disturbing the deposit. Carefully take the capsule off and the cork out, using one of the gentle dual-action corkscrews. Using a funnel, pour the wine slowly and steadily into the decanter. Do not stop half way: this allows the wine to flow back into the bottle and stir up the sludge. When you see black specks enter the funnel, stop. A well-placed light below the bottle neck helps: a candle is traditional but it does tend to singe the eyebrows. It is said that you can tell a true connoisseur, veteran of a thousand decantings, by his bushy eyebrows: they grow back faster if singed.

GLASSES

Beautiful fine crystal glasses can be bought that have been designed for specific wines: there is one type for old

burgundy, another for young. Most people worry more about the cost of replacing these glasses than the finer aesthetics of size and the precise shape.

The only vital thing about wine glasses is the basic shape. The glass should be tulip-shaped, with an inwards-turning rim, and it should have a reasonable stem. This shape helps direct the wine's aroma to your nose. Try a wine in an open-bowled glass and a tulip-shaped one: the aroma, and the pleasure, will be more intense with the tulip. Such a shape also allows the drinker to swirl the wine around, a process which releases more scents.

Glasses should be large enough to take a generous measure when only one-third full. This allows 'swirling' and avoids the wine becoming too warm as the drinker's hand holds it. (Hold a glass of white wine by the aforementioned stem, for the same reason.)

Clear glass is much better than cut, though cut glass does reflect the colour of wine attractively. Clear glasses allow us to see the colour more clearly, and they are far easier to keep clean. Do not use coloured glass, except for really informal meals where the wine is of little concern.

The real point about expensive crystal is its thinness. There is no doubt that really thin glass, with a fine rim, makes wine taste better. No-one is sure why, but it is true. So buy the finest glasses that your lifestyle, and your nerves, will allow.

TASTING WINE

Wine tasting began as a trade skill: merchants investing their cash in a cask, or shipload, of wine would judge it by tasting. Then suppliers began to assemble samples of several wines for customers to try, and the wine-tasting was born. Many people still taste as part of their job: merchants still appraise new wines, and routinely sample their own stock, and their competitors'. There are two reasons for this routine checking: wine will change over time, and batches of wine will vary. Journalists also taste widely in order to judge and write about wines, and judges at competitive tastings work hardest of all, appraising hundreds of wines and giving medals to the best.

There is much debate about scores. These are given by self-appointed wine critics such as writers, and by judging panels. Wines are rated out of 20, or 100, and when the results are published those which get higher marks tend to out-sell the lower. Any wine score, as the more candid critics agree, is a

Decanters and glasses: the tall glasses are for sparkling wine, the tulip-shaped ones are ideal for fine reds and whites.

mere snapshot. It reflects the state of the wine, and the taster, on one day. The wine will change, and so will the taster. Do not put too much weight upon these scores: try for yourself.

The third kind of tasting is that done by amateurs either to help them buy wine, or purely for its own sake. Learn the basic techniques and you will be able to judge wines quickly and surely. Many stores now offer wines for tasting, and an organised approach will allow a quick decision on quality and value. Tasting can go on to become a hobby, with groups getting together to try famous or rare wines, but the technique started as a buying tool and that is what it is most used for.

To learn to taste, free your mind of ideas about adjectives. There is no need to use, still less invent, arcane and idiotic words. The idea is simply to fix the taste in your memory, or in your notebook. Use words that mean something to you — and keep them to yourself. There are enough people publishing their tasting notes.

THE FOUR STAGES OF TASTING

Look at the wine, smell it, taste it (not forgetting to spit it out) then record your impressions. The smelling and the noting are the most important: some professionals do

nothing else, working down a row of bottles at high speed, nosing (as they call it) and scribbling.

COLOUR

Wines are either white or red. Unless they are rosé (pink). Or the sort of dark brown that signals sherry. Even within the basic colours there are enormous variations. Red wines can be pale and translucent, like a sun-filled stained glass window. Or they can be dark, almost black, and impossible to see through. Whites can be transparent, almost colourless, or a deep yellow like parchment.

Colour is a useful clue to style and taste, and to quality (which is why professional tasters look at the wine before tasting it). Any wine ought to be bright. It should shine in the glass: a dull, lifeless shade means the wine is just that. Look too to see if the wine is clear: haze or sediment are bad signs. Then check the depth of colour: pale or dark? Red wines should be deep and rich: light 'thin' colours, a watered-down look, spell a light and characterless wine.

All this becomes second nature as you grow to love wine, and hardly needs thinking about. The next steps in judging the wine are rather more considered and can be omitted if pure enjoyment, rather than considered appraisal, are what you have in mind.

Colour tells a lot about the age of the wine and its state of maturity, or lack of it. With the wine in a glass, look at the point where the surface of the pool of wine touches the glass: tasters call this the 'rim'. Is there a clear band around the wine? Does the red fade into orange or brown, or the yellow-white into browny-gold? All these are signs of age. Look into the heart of the glass: in a red wine, is there a hint of orange all the way in? Is the wine pale and clear? Again, an older wine — perhaps too old. In a white wine, suspect a dull, faded brown hue when you anticipated clear gold. Such a wine may be oxidized: the air may have got in round the cork and spoiled the wine.

USING YOUR SENSES

Wine is about taste. It is all very well looking at the colour, or smelling the bouquet, but taste is the biggie. There will indeed be plenty of times when wine is there for drinking, not thinking, and nothing should stand between you and your table companions and the flavours in the glass. But it is sometimes useful to stand a little back from the wine and appraise, as well as enjoy.

The key tool is your nose, or rather the organs of scent to which your nose conveys sensations. If you are after the subtleties, taste is a blunt instrument: your nose can detect for more nuances and evoke far more memories than your palate: despite all that talk about 'having a good palate', the saying should be 'having a good nose'.

If the nose is the key, the memory is the treasure-chest it unlocks. The point about the smell of a wine is twofold: first, it can tell you a lot about quality, character and condition. Second, and even more important, the smell can unlock memories. Brain scientists know that memory and smell are closely linked: think how a perfume or the scent of a flower reminds you of a special evening or a long-ago garden. Wine smells do the same: the scent of oak-wood, mint and spice that spells young Cabernet Sauvignon is stored away up there somewhere, and the first whiff from a glass of a similar wine will bring it out. To allow this happen, keep a clear head. Do not clutter it up with thoughts and preconceptions, do not expect anything. And (a different problem but just as real) keep away from strong scents such as tobacco and perfume.

Taste comes last, because the palate is the least subtle sense deployed. Take a good mouthful of the wine — and hold it in your mouth. Do not swallow, swill it around. Let it coat the tongue and the sides and roof of the mouth. Take note of the sensations, both on the palate and in the nose: the aromas will find their way to the olfactory nerve even from the mouth.

Finally, spit it out. This is an awful waste of wine (unless it is immature and undrinkable) but it is not possible to taste many wines if you swallow. This is because you will soon get drunk, or at least incapable of subtle taste judgment. And the palate seems to get tired more quickly if you swallow: without regular practice, it is hard to taste many wines anyway.

GUESSING ABOUT A WINE'S FUTURE

Hidden in the glass are clues to what the wine will taste like later on. With some wines there is not much future to worry about: there they are, ready to drink. This is true of the majority of wine, made and sold ready for the corkscrew. Some wines (see the cellar chapter) deserve to be kept. Spotting these is part of the job of the taster.

Red wines with a future in the cellar will show it in their colour: depth, even inkiness, is desirable. The nose may be 'dumb': winespeak for more or less non-existent — or you may just smell oak from the casks and/or ripe fruit. The palate will help spot the 'structure' of a cellar-worthy wine: you will note tannin, the mouth-puckering sensation, rather than taste, which is akin to drinking strong tea. There will be acidity, and a taste of ripe fruit underneath it all. The taster gambles that the tannins and acidity will soften, leaving the fruit and complexity of a mature, fine wine.

All tasters get it wrong: sometimes the entire world of wine falls over its feet about an entire vintage. Wines do not develop the way the books say they should do: different vintages, different châteaux, even different bottles, have their life pattern, much as do people.

That said, be prepared to back your judgment of a wine's potential, especially if a relatively inexpensive or obscure wine seems to have the structure for keeping. There are still plenty of pleasant surprises in store: not all the good wines have been found yet, and clever producers can conjure quality from the most unlikely places.

WINE WORDS

Words on labels, often in the language of the winemaker, may give useful clues to a wine's taste and style. F = French; G = German; I = Italian; P = Portuguese; S = Spanish.

Abboccato (I) Medium-sweet.

Adega (P) Winery.

Amabile (I) Sweet.

Appellation d'Origine Contrôlée (AOC) (F) Official classification: the top level of French wine.

Auslese (G) German wine, usually sweet, from selected bunches of very ripe grapes, picked late in the autumn.

Azienda agricola (I) Wine estate.

Beerenauslese (G) Rare, sweet German wine from selected, very ripe grapes.

Blanc de blancs (F) White wine from only white grapes — which is how 99% of whites are made, so a meaningless term. Also used (helpfully) to describe champagne made from Chardonnay.

Blanc de noirs (F) White wine made from black grapes.

Bottle-fermented Sparkling wine made by superior methods.

Branco (P) White.

Brut (F) Dry; used of champagne and other sparkling wines.

Brut nature (F) Very dry sparkling wine.

Château (F) Literally castle or country house; in wine a unit of land, which may not have a castle (or even a house), but which is run as a wine estate.

Clairet (F) Light red Bordeaux wine. Origin of the word 'claret'.

Classico (I) The best part of a wine area.

Crémant (F) Gently sparkling Champagne; elsewhere in France a sparkling wine made by the Champagne technique.

Cru Bourgeois (F) The class of Médoc château below Cru Classé.

Cru Classé Classed growth: in the Médoc, a château listed in the five ranks of the 1855 Classification.

Demi-sec (F) Medium-dry; but in champagne, medium-sweet.

Denominação de Origem Controlada (DOC) (P) The top rank of Portugal's quality wines.

Denominación de Origen (DO) (S) Spanish quality wine.

Denominación de Origen Calificada (DOC) (S) Top grade Spanish quality wines.

Denominazione di Origine Controllata (DOC) (I) Italian quality wine.

Denominazione di Origine Controllata e Garantita (DOCG) (I) Top grade Italian quality wine.

Doce (P) Sweet.

Domaine (F) Same as château; a wine estate.

Doux (F) Sweet.

Dulce (I and S) Sweet.

Eiswein (G) 'Ice-wine' from frozen grapes. Rich, concentrated and expensive. When grapes are pressed, the water in them remains as ice and the concentrated juice flows out.

Fattoria (I) Wine estate.

Frizzante (I) Slightly sparkling.

Garrafeira (P) Red wine aged for at least two years in cask and one in bottle.

Grand Cru (F) Top-quality French wine: but note that the term is used differently in Bordeaux, Burgundy, Champagne and Alsace.

Gran reserva (S) Red wines of very good vintages, aged at least two years in cask and three in bottle.

Halbtrocken (G) Medium-dry.

Indicação de Proveniencia Regulamentada (IPR) (P) The second rank of Portuguese quality wine.

Joven (S) Young.

Kabinett (G) The basic level of German QmP wines.

Landwein (G) Country wine, equivalent to Vin de Pays.

Liquoroso (I) Fortified dessert wine.

Metodo classico, metodo tradizionale (I) Sparkling wine made by the champagne method.

Moelleux (F) Sweet white wine.

Novello (I) New, like nouveau.

NV Non-vintage.

Paddock In Australia, a named vineyard.

Pajarete (S) Medium-sweet.

Passito (I) Sweet wine from dried grapes.

Pétillant (F) Gently sparkling.

Petit château (F) Bordeaux: an unclassified wine estate.

Podere (I) Wine estate.

Premier Cru (F) Officially-ranked vineyard or estate: top grade in Bordeaux, second in Burgundy.

Primeur (F) Wines made to be drunk very young.

Qualitätswein eines bestimmten Anbaugebietes (QbA) (G) The lower of two bands for German quality wine. Means 'quality wine from a specific region'.

Qualitätswein mit Prädikat (QmP) (G) 'Quality wine with distinction'. The higher German quality wine band. Wines made from grapes sweet enough to need no added sugar. Each QmP wine is placed in one of six sweetness levels: Kabinett; Spätlese; Auslese; Beerenauslese; Trockenbeerenauslese; Eiswein.

QbA, QmP (G) See above.

Quinta (P) Farm, estate.

Recioto (I) Sweet red wine from grapes that have been dried to concentrate their juice.

Reserva (S) Red wines: aged at least a year in cask, plus two in bottle. White and rosé: aged two years, at least six months in cask.

Rich Champagne: very sweet.

Rosado (S) Rosé.

Rosato (I) Rosé.

Riserva (I) DOC or DOCG wines with extra ageing.

Sec (F) Dry. For champagne, medium-dry.

Seco (S and P) Dry.

Secco (I) Dry.

Sélection de grains nobles (F) Alsace: wines from late-picked grapes with noble rot or naturally dried, and thus very sweet.

Sin crianza (S) Not aged in oak

Solar (P) Château, wine estate.

Spätlese (G) 'Late-picked'; late-harvest QmP wine, usually sweet.

Spumante (I) Sparkling.

Superiore (I) Wine with extra alcohol or longer ageing.

Sur lie (F) (Especially Muscadet) bottled without being racked.

Tafelwein (G) Table wine, the lowest German grade. Deutscher Tafelwein means the wine is actually from Germany.

Tenuta (I) Wine estate.

Tinto (S and P) Red.

Trocken (G) Dry wine. Not, however:

Trockenbeerenauslese (G) The highest, rarest grade of German wine, always sweet and intense. Made from individually selected overripe grapes with noble rot.

Vendange tardive (F) In Alsace, late-harvest wine, usually sweet.

Vigna (I) Vineyard.

Vigneto (I) Vineyard.

Vin Délimité de Qualité Supérieure (VDQS) (F) Second grade of French quality wine.

Vin de pays (F) Country wine, made under rules about grapes and localities.

Vin de table (F) The lowest grade of French wine.

Vin doux naturel (VDN) (F) Sweet, fortified wine.

Vino da tavola (I) Table wine. Some are quality wines made in DOC areas but not according to DOC rules.

Vino de crianza (S) Quality wine with two years' ageing, a minimum of six months in cask.

Vino joven (S) Young, or un-aged, wine.

Vino de mesa (VdM) (S) Basic Spanish table wine.

Vino de la tierra (VdT) (S) Country wine, like vin de pays.

THE WORLD OF WINE

Where in the world does wine belong? Everywhere that it rains, at least in the winter, and does not freeze too hard or grow too hot. Vineyards are to be found in Canada, overlooking the Great Lakes; in Zimbabwe, not far south of the Equator, and in India, not far north of it. There are 50 countries in the world where grapes are grown to make wine. That said, the grape vine is most at home in the zones where the climate is close to that of the Mediterranean, or perhaps a little cooler. The world map shows two clear bands of wine countries: one in each hemisphere. The northern wine trail follows the 40° North parallel of latitude from southern Europe across the Black Sea and then, after a great gap eastwards, reappears in China and Japan, then crosses the Pacific to California, and emerges again on the East Coast of the USA. South of the Equator, 40° South runs close to the vineyards of Chile and Argentina, beside those of South Africa, just below Australia's main vine country and through New Zealand.

Vines in the Napa Valley, California.

WHERE WINE BEGAN

WILD GRAPES, PICKED FROM vines looping through the forest, were doubtless among the foodstuffs early humans gathered. Their sweetness would have made them welcome, probably sought after. At some point in time, in some early settlement, people started to cultivate the vine — and, perhaps somewhat earlier, human beings made wine, by accident, from ripe grapes. Why grapes, among all the fruits of the forest? Grapes bring with them the ingredients of wine: sweet juice, containing natural sugars, and yeast. The yeasts live on the skins of the grapes: once the grapeskins burst open, due to over-ripeness or through deliberate crushing, they can get at the juice. Providing the grapes are in a container, and the juice is thus confined, fermentation will begin.

THE MAGIC OF WINE

Early peoples thought that fermentation was the work of the gods. Indeed, the magic is still potent: crushed ripe grapes turn, in a frothing mass, into a delicious and intoxicating liquid. In ancient Babylon, Egypt, Rome and Greece, and in a hundred other cultures whose history we do not know, wine was considered the gift of the gods. Its effects — drunkenness — were a glimpse of the divine. Other cultures, such as China, discovered and made wine, but did not elevate it to such a status. The native American civilizations never discovered wine at all.

It is to the eastern Mediterranean that we owe wine. The peoples and rulers of the lands from Egypt round through Palestine and Syria to Turkey and Greece, and eastwards in Babylon and Armenia, all grew grapes and made wine. They perfected styles of wine made to this day, they established trade in wine which still goes on, they wrote about it and we still read their thoughts.

The heroes of Greece drank wine at their victory feasts, the citizens of sophisticated Athens at their dinner parties. The wines of favoured islands and regions were traded far across the sea: divers still find cargoes of clay wine jars — *amphorae* — to show that trade was hazardous, and wine well prized. Egypt's Pharaohs planted royal vineyards and their stewards carefully labelled the wines according to their origin and vintage, much as we do now. Egypt imported wine from Syria and the area which is now Lebanon; Babylon went for wine to the hills of what is now eastern Turkey.

IN THE CLASSICAL TASTE

What was ancient wine like? We read that it was usual to dilute it: was this because the wine was unpleasant, or very strong? Probably the latter: wine was thought best when powerful, concentrated and sweet. The nearest equivalent today is the pungent, almost black, wine that is made in the Jerez district of Spain and used for sweetening and colouring blends of sherry. There are some Mediterranean wines which can be said to be relics of classical taste. Commandaria from Cyprus, Malaga from Spain, some of the Vin Santo from Italy, Mavro from the Greek islands: all are of a type, deep and rich in taste and texture. There are instructions in Greek and Roman texts for the making of wines from dried grapes, a practice still known today all over the Mediterranean. Such a wine is

Left: treading grapes in Roman times, from a mosaic found in Tunisia.
Top right: the Roman world.

indeed sweet, long-lasting, and tolerant of storage. It does not spoil like a light wine when exposed to air. And it tastes good diluted. Whether we would enjoy following classical authors in diluting wines with sea water is doubtful.

THE BIBLE AND THE ROMANS

The Old Testament of the Bible is rich in references to wine; as an article of trade, as a desirable pleasure — but not as part of religion. It was Christianity which established the link between wine and God as a part of the Sacrament.

Christianity grew up in conflict, then in concert, with Rome, which had learned from Greece of the pleasures of wine. Italy was even more the vine's natural home than the countries of the Near East. Roman writers left us manuals of vine growing, lists of great estates and vintages, and Roman colonists the germs of great vineyards as far north as the Moselle — see map above. As Rome's empire expanded, the soldiers and traders planted vines to give them the wine that was part of their familiar diet. Hungary, Romania, the Rhine, Burgundy, even Britain have vineyards today on sites chosen by the Romans.

Christianity, organised by its priests and bishops, outlived the secular power of Rome's emperors and legions. The Dark Ages of Europe, when no authority could outbid the barbarian sword, saw churches alone preserve shreds of Roman order. With the church came the vineyards; making altar wine, then also wine as a readily-tradeable and durable commodity that enriched abbeys and cathedrals. So many of the vineyards revered by connoisseurs today were planted by monks: Clos Vougeot in Burgundy, the great sites of the Rheingau, some of the best parts of the Marne Valley in Champagne. Some still have the walls the monks built.

WINE'S PLACE IN HISTORY

Behind this continuous pursuit of wine was not only religion, and the search for pleasure — but sheer necessity. Until the 20th century, and not even then in some places, water was a dangerous beverage. Towns with clean water supplies were rare: most people had to cope with contaminated water. Wine, added to water, acts as a disinfectant and renders doubtful supplies palatable. Wine was also a part of the diet

Cork, which became the main material for stoppering bottles in the 18th century, is still the mainstay of wine. It is stripped from the bark of cork oaks, as here in southern Spain.

of both ancient and medieval communities. Typically sweet, classical wine offered a reviving dose of sugar, most welcome after a long hot day. Wine too was a staple medicine and the cleanser of wounds. The lengths to which our ancestors went to acquire wine are explained if it is thought of not just as a drink, but as foodstuff, a medicine and a purifier.

CASKS, CORKS AND BOTTLES

Wine also had the knack of keeping. Water, even beer, would spoil if kept in a jar or cask for long. Wine could be expected to last some months. Roman wines, sealed in *amphorae* or casks, lasted for decades. However wine in a wooden cask, especially a leaky medieval one, will spoil if it is not kept well stoppered. If wine is drawn from the cask, air gets in and the remaining wine will, sooner or later, turn to vinegar. Bottles were known to the Romans, but the idea of bottling wine to keep it for long periods dates back only three hundred years. Before then, all wine was shipped, sold and stored in casks. A large cask's contents was frequently divided on arrival among several small ones, to delay the spoilage of the wine by broaching smaller

amounts at a time. But the keeping qualities of medieval wine are shown by the reversal of our idea that old wine is better than new. Medieval wine was best when young: age turned it sour. Thus wine prices rose when a new vintage came in, and fell in the spring and summer as the wine deteriorated.

The great change came in the late 17th and early 18th centuries. To this period we can trace the birth of fine wine. The twin developments that were its parents were mass-produced bottles and corks. Corks were used by the Romans but — as with central heating — this knowledge was forgotten for centuries. The glass bottle changed more: known as ornamental serving vessels, they were too fragile for shipping and storage until an English inventor worked out how to fire glass-making furnaces with coal, not wood. The fires grew hotter, the resulting glass stronger. Add corks, and the winemakers had the means to bottle their wines. Cork is the perfect stopper: it is easy to cut to shape, yet when compressed and inserted into the bottle neck it springs out to completely seal the bottle. Wine could henceforth be kept in bottle, and wine lovers began to find that wine changed, indeed improved, if kept.

Champagne was the region which gained most from the bottle/cork combination. It allowed the natural effervescence of the wine to be captured behind a wired-down cork.

The use of corks encouraged the process of refinement in wine making: if a wine was to be kept, it had to be good; and good wine deserved maturing. The ancient Romans and the medieval monks had been careful, perfectionist vine growers and winemakers; now the landowners of 18th century France, Italy and Germany applied the same care and skill to their wines. The aim was to capture the markets in the great cities which began to grow up in northern Europe. In London, Amsterdam, Paris and Copenhagen, and in a hundred other towns and a thousand country mansions, people were growing rich from trade and agriculture. They demanded the best and most refined and the rarest: their houses, pictures and furniture are monuments to their taste.

People living today have tasted wines from this first golden age of modern winemaking. Bottles survive in the cellars of châteaux in Bordeaux, and of country houses in Britain, which date from the 1780s. These wines can still be great today — though on opening, their taste and aroma vanish quickly as time catches up with them. These wines would not exist without the humble cork.

EUROPE & THE NEW WORLD

THE WORLD'S WINE LANDS DIVIDE into Europe and the rest. The European vineyards have as close neighbours the Mediterranean wine lands and those of the Black Sea; all these are covered in the first half of this section. The rest of the world — the Americas, Australasia, southern Africa — is often called the 'New World' of wine. It is covered from page 102 onwards. All these continents gained wine as part of the process of European exploration and colonisation. Today they make wines that compete with, and complement, those of the European motherland. Asia's vineyards, in China, Japan and India, have an older and separate tradition: they are discussed on pages 125–6.

As described above, Europe's vineyards effectively began with the Romans, though the eastern Mediterranean world owes more to the Greeks. Greek colonists took the vine with them to Sicily and southern France, through the straits to the Black Sea, and as far as the Crimea and the Danube. Before vines arrived, the taste of wine was known to half-civilized tribes as far north as Britain: wine was a staple of trade.

Much effort has been spent in trying to trace the great grape varieties around the world. Despite scholarly labours the story is still speculation. The Rhône's Syrah vine may have come from Persia via the Greeks, or this may be a misapprehension based upon its alternative name, Shiraz. The Cabernet family may have its antecedents in Roman Bordeaux, but on the other hand the name Cabernet is a fairly recent one.

What is clear is the modern spread of grape varieties and wine styles, mostly outward from France. The list of classic grapes is essentially French: only Riesling, which is German (though planted in France), comes from elsewhere. The French classic vines are now planted virtually everywhere wine is made, to the confusion of the French, to whom the grape variety is not the most important thing about a wine.

Wine districts of Europe stretch from Portugal to the Ukraine.

The styles of French wine, as established over the last 150 years, have also become the templates for winemakers virtually everywhere.

This is why this Atlas begins with France. You may not drink much, if any, French wine. But the wine you do drink will often be made from French varieties of grapes, and be made by people who know and imitate French styles.

EUROPE'S WINE ZONES

Northern Europe, from roughly the latitude of the English Channel (51°N) northward, is too cool for grapes to ripen. Indeed, only exceptional sites north of Paris (49°N) have the capacity to regularly yield wine. Such places are the warm, sunny south-facing slopes of river valleys in Germany, the carefully chosen chalk slopes of Champagne. Latitude equals intensity of sunshine — the angle of the sun, and thus its warmth, grows less as you move north. But there are other factors. In the far west of Europe, Atlantic winds bring rain and cloud, lessening the amount of sun but decreasing also the risk of winter frost. In the east, from the Rhine onwards, hard winters become more of a threat, while summers are drier and sunnier. This change can be seen between Bordeaux, in the west of France, and Burgundy in the east. Bordeaux, close to the ocean, has much more winter rain, but warmer winter temperatures. Averages hide the unusual, though: in 1991, and in 1956, Bordeaux was devastated by spring frosts which even its maritime location could not prevent.

Further south, altitude becomes a factor in the placing of vineyards. The best Chianti estates, in central Italy, are around 500m (1,650ft) above sea level. Here the summer heat is moderated by the mountain breezes.

Styles of wine vary with location. The cool, northern vineyards, such as the Loire, Champagne and the Rhine, nearly always yield white wines as the amount of sun is not great enough to ripen black grapes to make red wine. In the south, in places such as southern Spain and Sicily, it is hard to make delicate white wines because grapes quickly become over-ripe, and due to the heat they lose acidity and flavour. These are the lands of red and fortified wines.

WHERE WINE ZONES ARE AND WHY

Climate has a lot to do with where vines are grown, as does (surprisingly) ancient history. More recent events have also played their part. The great vine blight, phylloxera, which swept Europe in the second half of the 19th century, devastated vineyards everywhere. Many were replanted using resistant rootstocks (brought, like the pest itself, from America) but some vineyards never reappeared. These included large tracts in northern Burgundy which were made redundant by the railway: cheap wine from the south could now be brought by train to Paris. Phylloxera was a boon to Rioja in northern Spain, and to the Lebanon, both of which prospered by supplying wine to France when many French vineyards were out of production.

Politics and frontiers have a bearing upon vineyards. Alsace, part of Germany from 1870 to 1918, was viewed by Germans as a bulk wine region. France, regaining control, encouraged the quality wines of the province. The wine lands of eastern Europe spent four decades, until 1989, satisfying the thirst of the former USSR for cheap, sweet wine. When that market dried up, they had to switch their sights onto the west, which demanded quite different styles of wine.

Europe still makes too much wine, and some of it, from southern Italy, Spain and southern France, is still below the standard which consumers are prepared to accept. But the story of Europe's wine in the last decades of the 20th century is one of success: many classic vineyards have expanded and further improved their standards, obscure but interesting wines are being made in greater quantity, and everyday wine is a great leap better and more reliable than ever before.

THE NEW WORLD

Vine cuttings were in the cargoes of exploring and colonising ships from Europe from 1492 onwards. First Mexico and the rest of Spanish America, then South Africa, then Australia, the USA and New Zealand acquired the vine. Today their wines are shipped back to Europe as part of a world-wide trade in wine: the finest wines from France are prized in America and the Far East; novel names and flavours from the New World brighten tables in Europe.

A wine atlas a generation ago would have been an atlas of Europe, with a patronising nod to local vineyards in other continents. Now, the classic wines of the New World are being created, and their vineyards take their rightful place beside Europe's classics on the world map.

WINE REGIONS OF FRANCE

Elegant châteaux epitomise French wine.

EVERY ACCOUNT OF THE WORLD'S WINE LANDS must begin with France. France may not be the winner on quantity of wine produced — Italy takes that honour in most years — but in terms of quality and variety France has no rival. France makes the most famous wines in the world, and — if wine was to have something as simple as a 'top ten', the best ones. It is important though to realise that not all French wine is good just because it has France on the label. If France makes the world's top wines — though she has more competitors for this title than formerly — she also comes up with some rather poor ones. This is perhaps inevitable given the vast scale and intricacy of the wine business in France. There are few corners of the southern two-thirds of this large country where vines do not grow. Some areas are world-renowned as sources of fine wine: Champagne, Bordeaux and Burgundy are the leading trio. In other parts, the wine is made to be drunk locally, and a visit from a merchant or wine lover from outside the county is a rare event. Then there is the great middle rank — the Loire, the Rhône, Alsace, the South — producing good-value wines with individuality and style. France is a wonderful country to explore, both on the ground, via the country roads and the tasting rooms of the châteaux, and via wine lists. Despite a certain standardisation, there are still many, many individual wines waiting to be discovered.

The reasons for the pre-eminence of France lie in geography. The country has a moderate climate, with only the north too cold for viticulture. The great river valleys of France provide a wide range of sites, soils and local climates. This means that just about every style of wine is made, from cool fresh whites and austere sparkling wines in the north, to sweet dessert wines and warming reds in the south. The history of France, too, has made its contribution: the Romans established many of the current vineyard zones, and every generation since has adapted and improved them.

Two thousand years of continuous development has allowed France to breed and nurture the classic vine varieties of the world, and to perfect the styles of wine which everyone wants to imitate. The red wines of Bordeaux and Burgundy, the sparkling wines of Champagne, and a dozen others are the patterns winemakers follow in California, Australia and most other wine lands. They do so through growing these classic grapes, and by adopting techniques invented and refined in France. Cabernet Sauvignon and Chardonnay, the two most successful grape 'exports', are so ubiquitous now that some New World wine drinkers do not realise their connection with France. But only a couple of generations ago they were the local vines of red bordeaux and white burgundy respectively, without the world-wide fame that has come since. Techniques like barrel-ageing for red wines, and the champagne method of making sparkling wine, have been taken up around the world.

France has been to some extent the victim of success: the imitators have become competitors. In response the French point to their unique climate, soils and vineyard sites: the individual mix, specific to each place, that they call *terroir*. No California or South African vineyard can duplicate French *terroir*, they assert.

THE RULES OF FRENCH WINE

The *terroir* concept is at the root of French wine law. A wine gets an official birth certificate, an *appellation d'origine contrôlée* (AOC), if (in the judgement of experts) it represents a local tradition of quality. The AOC sets out the grapes allowed, the techniques to be used, the yield permitted. With an AOC there may be smaller, more restrictive AOCs for higher-quality wines. Thus within the Cotes du Rhône AOC are a handful of villages considered better than the rest. These can add '-Villages' to the simple AOC. More humble wines are either called *vins de pays* (country wines) or just *vins de table*. *Vins de pays* can be very good value. Many of the most go-ahead wine producers in Southern France use these names as they free them from the rules and restrictions of an AOC. A *vin de pays* label confers a wider choice of grape varieties: Cabernet or Merlot reds, and Sauvignon and Chardonnay whites, can be made in zones where the AOC (if any) does not permit them.

More confusion is generated by the terms '*grand cru*' and '*premier cru*' than anything else about French wine. *Cru* means both vineyard, a specific plot, and the wine made from it. The terms are used differently in the various vineyard zones. Bordeaux speaks of a '*grand cru*' and means the least important grade of château in St-Emilion; Burgundy lists its handful of top vineyards as '*grand cru*'. But Burgundy does not use the words '*grand cru*' on the label....

The idea of a château is another trap for the unwary. Château does indeed translate as castle, but set aside thoughts of a grand estate making lordly wine. In Bordeaux, and many other areas, anything can be a château. All the word means is a wine-growing farm. The wine does not even have to be made there — though the law on this aspect is being tightened: there is now an official list of châteaux in Bordeaux, with 10,000 properties on it.

In Bordeaux labels sometimes carry the words *cru classé*, showing that the wine was awarded a place in one of the official classifications. The Médoc classification was carried out in 1855, so it is questionable whether it still holds much meaning. Sauternes dates from the same year; St-Emilion's is revised every ten years; Graves has a list dating from 1959.

The best guarantee of quality and value is the name of the maker. AOC acts as a filter which removes really bad wine, but it cannot force everyone to make good wine. The thousands of growers and merchants who put their names on the bottles include some who want to build reputations, and others who are incompetent or lazy. If you find one that makes good wine, ask for it again. Be prepared to experiment with vins de pays: these are the good-value country wines. Alternatively, find a merchant who can select French wine and take his or her advice. But that will be to miss half the pleasure of French wine, which comes from exploration of its almost infinite variety.

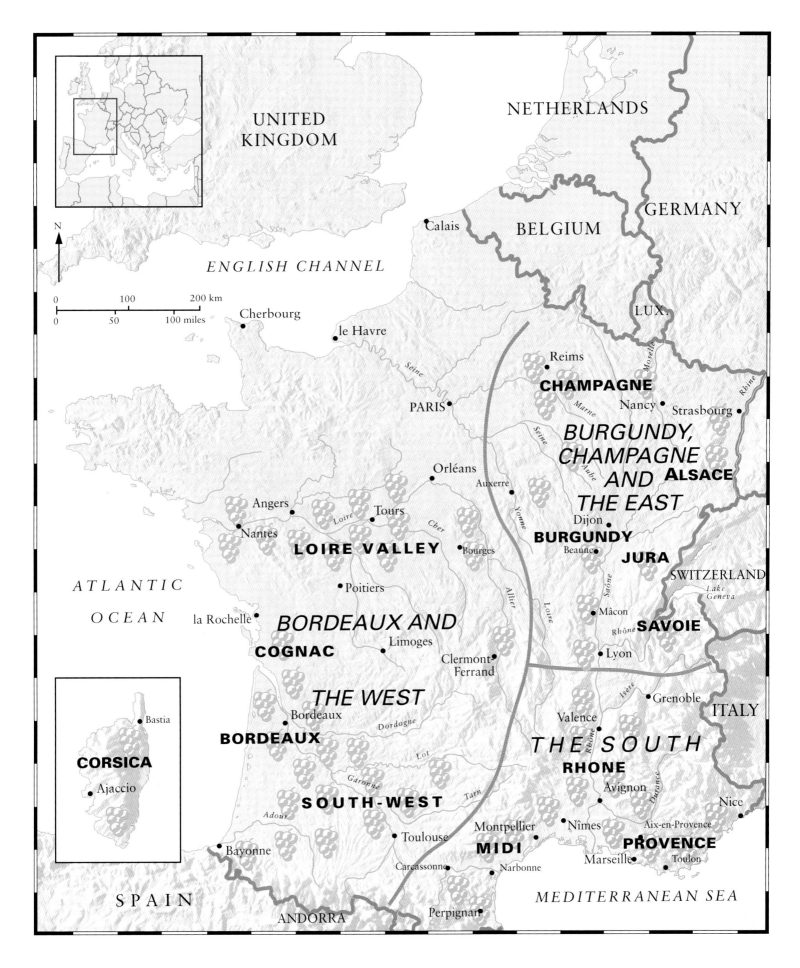

BORDEAUX & THE WEST

THE SOFT ATLANTIC LIGHT of western France bathes the vineyards and châteaux of Bordeaux and the Loire, while the rain brought by the ocean winds fills the many rivers which carve their way through this beautiful, intensely pastoral, landscape. Wine is made in nearly every valley from the mighty River Loire to the mountains of the Pyrenees. Further north, Brittany and Normandy are too cold; further east, the vineyards are mere pockets amid the rocky hills of central France.

The broad band of Loire vineyards spreads halfway across France along the river and its tributaries. Here most wines are white: only perhaps three years in ten will there be the warmth for really ripe reds. Further south, a wide tract of vines yield thin white wine for distilling into Cognac. South again comes the Bordeaux region, where the great rivers Dordogne and Garonne sweep down from the hills, combining to form the still greater Gironde. Here it is a vital few degrees warmer, and red wines come into their own. The ocean still moderates the climate, however, and Médoc and St-Emilion fear a cool summer more than a grape-shrivelling heat wave.

Both Bordeaux and Loire wines have been traded by sea for a thousand years. Their tastes have been shaped by the thirsts of northern Europe as well as by their climate and soils. The medieval cities of London, Amsterdam and Copenhagen consumed Bordeaux's red wines and the Loire's whites in great amounts. Paris and the rest of inland France drew its wine from Burgundy and the east. These habits have lasted to this day: Bordeaux exports much of its best wine, as far away as the Americas and the East. The wines from inland of Bordeaux, from zones such as Cahors and Gaillac, have equally long histories, but they suffered from the dominance of the Bordeaux merchants, who denied the 'up-country' wines free passage to the outside world. Now that roads not rivers form the trade routes, these wines, grouped under the name Southwest France, are finding markets more readily.

The wine zones on this map share a climate in common, and also share many of the same grape varieties. White wines are made from Sauvignon Blanc in Bordeaux and in the Sancerre and Touraine regions of the Loire. Reds made from the Cabernet family of grapes are found in Bordeaux, the Loire and in patches across the South-west.

While this tract of France makes wines of virtually every style, they have a common identity drawn from the cool, fresh climate. These are refreshing wines, not heavy ones; brisk and light to taste, not rich and unctuous. The exceptions are the famous sweet white wines of Sauternes, in Bordeaux. These, and their lesser-known cousins from the Loire, are made from very ripe, intensely sweet grapes in only the warmest of autumns.

Winemakers around the world find in western France examples to aim at. The modern renaissance of California was to a large extent prompted by the desire of pioneer growers to emulate the great red Bordeaux wines, using Cabernet Sauvignon and other grapes grown in the Napa Valley and elsewhere. In New Zealand, winemakers have succeeded in making white wines from Sauvignon Blanc that rival their prototypes from Pouilly and Sancerre on the Loire.

The turetted château of Pichon-Longueville-Baron, in Pauillac, one of the grandest wine estates in Bordeaux.

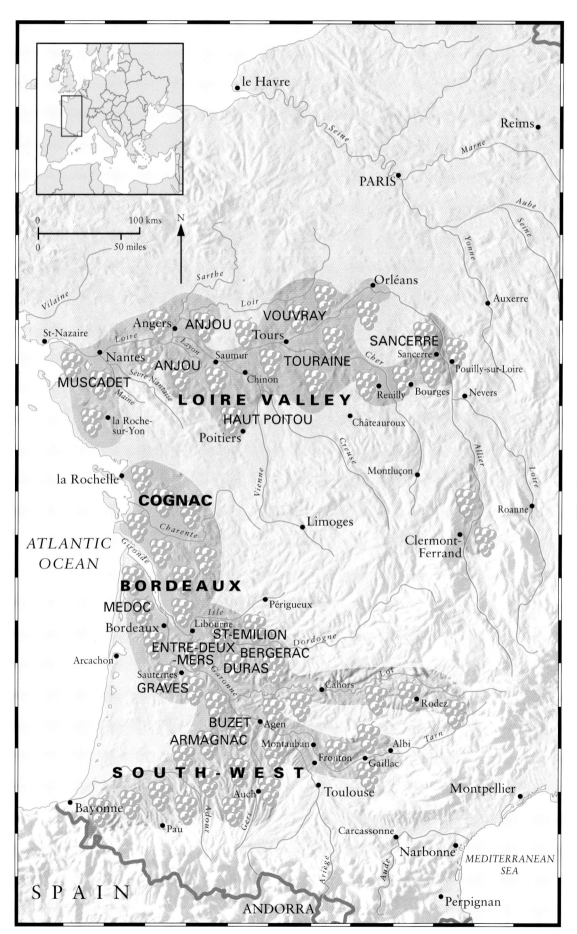

New oak casks are a major purchase each year when making high-quality wine in Bordeaux. These await filling with new wine at Château la Louvière, Léognan, Graves.

BORDEAUX

Bordeaux is the capital city of a province, the *département* of the Gironde, devoted to wine. At the heart of the city are the warehouses which store the casks ready for shipping. All around are the great vineyards of the Médoc, Graves, St-Emilion and the other famous names. Thousands of wine estates, called châteaux, dot the vineyards, producing enormous amounts of wine, both white and red. The reds are traditionally known in English as claret. They range from the great classed growths to minor wines from '*petits châteaux*'. Whites include the great sweet Sauternes and the dry wines of Graves and Entre-Deux-Mers.

THE MÉDOC

The Gironde estuary splits Bordeaux's vineyards in half, leading wine lovers to talk about 'Right Bank' wines from St-Emilion and thereabouts, with the Médoc and Graves as 'Left Bank' (though that term is less used). All districts grow (in varying proportions) the Cabernet Sauvignon, Merlot and Cabernet Franc vines for reds, and Sauvignon Blanc and Sémillon for whites.

Château Carbonnieux, a leading estate in the Graves region of Bordeaux, comes under the top Pessac-Léognan appellation.

When wine lovers think of great red wines, the names of a string of unassuming French villages come to mind. Margaux and Pauillac, St-Julien and St-Estèphe: these are the sites of the great wine châteaux of the Médoc. Here, in gentle countryside as unremarkable as any in the world of wine, are the names that grace a thousand wine lists: Latour, Beychevelle, Palmer, Lafite, Mouton.

Visitors to the Médoc find it hard to credit the excitement. Can this be the home of great wine? The country is flat, with tidy vineyards interspersed with rather damp cow pastures and the occasional patch of woodland. The horizons are wide, with glimpses of a broad, brown river: the Gironde. The glamour comes from the scattering of grey, stone-built châteaux, each with its grand entrance of pillars and gates. The gravel courtyards are precisely raked, flags fly, carefully tended beds are bright with flowers.

The châteaux are the headquarters of the great wine estates. Around them stand the vineyards, with low-growing Cabernet

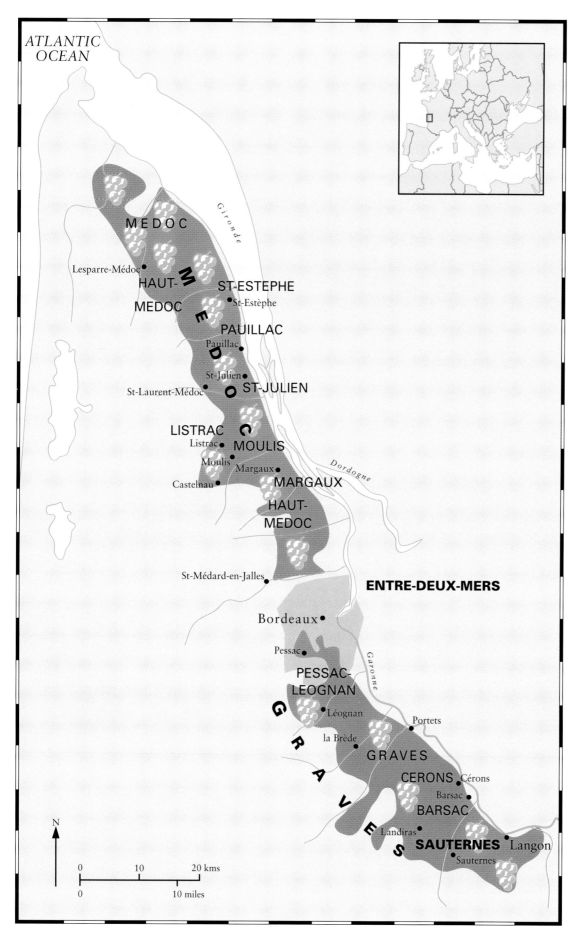

ATLANTIC OCEAN

MEDOC

Lesparre-Médoc

HAUT-MEDOC

ST-ESTEPHE
St-Estèphe

PAUILLAC
Pauillac

St-Julien
St-Laurent-Médoc ST-JULIEN

M E D O C

LISTRAC
Listrac MOULIS
Moulis Margaux
Castelnau MARGAUX

HAUT-MEDOC

St-Médard-en-Jalles

ENTRE-DEUX-MERS

Bordeaux

Pessac

PESSAC-LEOGNAN
Léognan Portets
la Brède

G R A V E S

GRAVES

CERONS Cérons

Barsac

BARSAC

Landiras

SAUTERNES Langon
Sauternes

Gironde

Dordogne

Garonne

N

0   10   20 kms

0   10 miles

The soil in the best Graves vineyards is, appropriately, gravel — the French word for which is 'graves'. Here at Château Haut-Brion, Cabernet Sauvignon grapes are ripening perfectly.

The Médoc and Graves vineyards line the left banks of the Gironde and Garonne rivers.

and Merlot vines, severely pruned. Beside and behind the château are the *cuverie* — the vat-house where the wine is made — and the *chai*: a great barn, sometimes part sunk in the ground, filled with a regiment of oak barrels. Here the wine ages before it is bottled, at perhaps two years old. In Bordeaux, winemaking is all splendidly self-contained. The fruit from the vineyards is slowly transformed into bottled wine: farming and processing all on the same estate.

These wines are some of the most expensive in the world. Why? Because for three centuries, sometimes more, the Médoc estates have proved that they can make red wine that ages into something sublime. Great Médoc wines can last for decades, slowly revealing their subtleties as the years go by.

Not all Médoc wine is great. The hierarchy is clear: the 61 classed growths, with the cherished right to print 'cru classé' on their labels, stand at the head. Even within this elite there are grades: only five châteaux are 'first growths'. The others cluster in descending ranks from second down to fifth. Next in the order come the *cru bourgeois* wines. There are about 300 of these. Other wines, many excellent, may carry only the name of their village, or merely 'Médoc'.

Very nearly all wine here is red. Most of it (especially the grander sort) needs time in bottle to show at its best. Vintages matter, too, for some years are too cool and rainy to make really good wine. A classed-growth Médoc is at its best from 8-20 years old, depending upon château and vintage. *Cru bourgeois* wines are worth trying from three years old, though most will keep well into their teens.

The Médoc taste moves from austere, even astringent in youth — the legacy of those oak casks, in part — to seductive, silky, even sublime in maturity. These are not opulent wines, lacking the ripe, fruity power of a New World Cabernet, nor are they perfumed and sweet in the way Burgundy can be. A good Médoc is wine to make you think. And, needless to say, it partners food beautifully, being balanced in its acidity and fruitiness.

GRAVES

Graves in French means 'gravel' — a clue to the soil and also to the high quality of the wine it produces. The Graves district is south of the Médoc, on the other side of the city of Bordeaux. Here, the woods are denser and the vineyards more patchy. Suburbs and straggling villages interrupt the vineyards. The red wines from here are softer, a little richer, sometimes earthier, than Médocs. They can be just as good: some would say that Château Haut-Brion, the leading Graves estate, is in some years the best red Bordeaux of all. The top châteaux are in the Pessac-Léognan district. In the wider Graves zone are many minor estates which offer good value.

Not all Graves is red: here, white wines make up nearly half the crop. These range from classic, expensive bottles on a par in stature with white Burgundy, to rather ordinary wines. Even minor white Graves is a lot better than it used to be, however. Modern winemaking has worked its wonders, and wine lovers are rediscovering the region. The grapes used are Sauvignon Blanc, as grown in the Loire, and Sémillon. They combine to make white wines which have brisk, refreshing flavours and a backbone which allows them to mature well.

SAUTERNES

Amid the Graves vineyards is a district where sweet white wines are a speciality. This is Sauternes, which with its neighbouring village Barsac and three other communes makes some of the most expensive, luscious wine in the world. The habit here is to delay picking the grapes until lingering autumn warmth has ripened them to honeyed sweetness. Growers here hope for something that others dread: the appearance on the grapes of sticky, grey mould. Not just any mould, however. This particular fungus, called *botrytis cinerea*, or 'noble rot', appears in warm, misty autumns. The locality, with its little rivers and hills, prompts mists, but these are not predictable and neither is the noble rot. When it occurs it shrivels the grape skins, letting the water in the juice evaporate: this concentrates the sweetness and flavour. To make top-class Sauternes means picking the grapes not in one sweep, but in several, taking only the ripest grapes each time. This costs far more than straightforward harvesting — and yields are much lower. Thus Sauternes is expensive. If it is too cheap, expect ordinary sweet wine without the sugar-and-spice complexity of real Sauternes.

No-one is sure when to drink Sauternes. The obvious idea of 'sweet with sweet' does not necessarily work. It quarrels with sweet deserts, declares a truce with plain, soft fruits such as peaches. Try it the French way: they adore it with foie gras and Roquefort cheese. Perhaps it is best drunk on its own, nicely chilled, with maybe a sweet biscuit to nibble.

ST-EMILION

The honey-coloured town of St-Emilion has the easy charm of a place that knows it has bewitched visitors for hundreds of years. The medieval streets are lined with shops and cafés, the little square with tables and umbrellas. Looking beyond the picturesque, the character of the town has quite a lot to tell about the quality of the local wine.

St-Emilion is built from limestone, quarried from the low but pronounced hill upon which the town stands. This hill is really the edge of a plateau of limestone which stretches north, east and west of the town. The edge of this giant slab of rock provides the south-facing, well-drained slopes that best suit vines in this relatively cool corner of western France. Along the slope — known as 'the Côte' — stand the châteaux of Belair, Ausone, Magdelaine, Pavie and a dozen others.

On the plateau, to the north, stand many more wine estates of varying fame. Indeed, it is hard to find a gap in the

Left: winter in St-Emilion: burning the vine prunings. The château in the background is Clos des Jacobins. Below: the Libournais zone lies east of Bordeaux

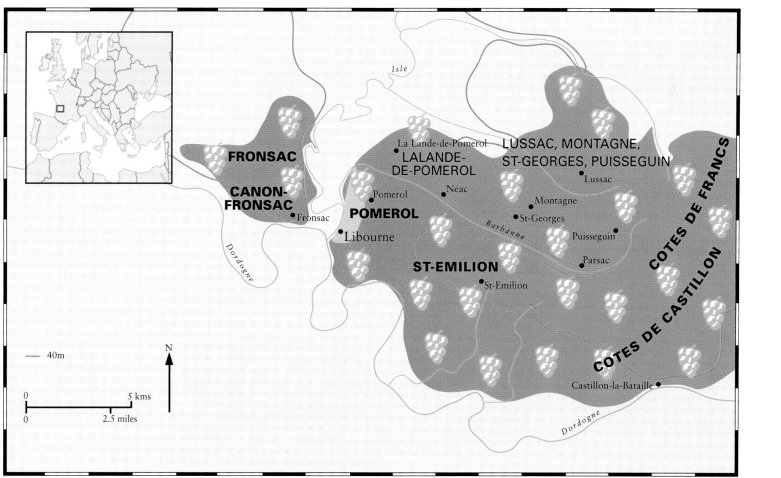

vines all the way from the low ground south of St-Emilion, on the banks of the River Dordogne, to beyond Pomerol to the north-west. The Côte does not have a monopoly of great wine in St-Emilion. Over to the north-west, almost in Pomerol, is Château Cheval Blanc, with one of the largest vineyards and the highest repute.

The wine of St-Emilion is red, and for once its character is truly told by its popular reputation. It is softer, fleshier, sweeter than the Médoc wines, earlier to mature (except from the greatest châteaux) and perhaps easier to enjoy. The character comes from the Merlot grape: a junior partner in the Médoc, but here dominant. Cabernet Franc, again a minor part of the Médoc recipe, is here almost as common as the Merlot. These grapes are grown because they better suit the conditions here. It is a little cooler, being further inland, and Merlot helpfully ripens earlier. The drawback is that it buds earlier too, making it vulnerable to spring frosts.

There are nearly 1,000 wine-producing estates in St-Emilion. Not all make their own wine: several hundred use the winemaking facilities of the cooperative. But there are enough names with their own labels to confuse even the most assiduous connoisseur. To add to the muddle there is a classification system that works upwards from *grand cru*. The *grands crus* here are fairly ordinary, though properties so rated have to meet certain standards and the list is revised every year. There are about 200 *grands cru*s. The next rung up is *grand cru classé*: these wines are tasted by a panel of experts. There are 63 of these — the list is revised every ten years or so.

The top St-Emilions are the dozen or so *premiers grands crus classés*. Even in this top rank there is a complication: two châteaux, Ausone and Cheval Blanc, are rated as 'A', the rest 'B'. These two properties are informally grouped with the five Médoc and Graves 'firsts' (see p46), Yquem in Sauternes and Pétrus in Pomerol in a top nine of Bordeaux.

Ordinary St-Emilion (and that covers quite a few wines with *grand cru* on the label) can be a lovely drink at 3–5 years old. Drink it just slightly chilled. The more serious wines age well and can be kept for 10–15 years. On the whole, St-Emilions give more pleasure young than do Médocs.

POMEROL

A minor road divides the vineyards of St-Emilion's Cheval Blanc from those of Pomerol's l'Evangile. There is little else to distinguish them — except reputation. Pomerol has come from obscurity to a prominence that must cause some gnashing of teeth in the much bigger St-Emilion appellation. Pomerol's fame trickles down from that of Pétrus, its first growth, a château whose wine is the most expensive red bordeaux of all. Several of the small estates here aspire to superstar status alongside Pétrus: Certan de May, Lafleur, Trotanoy and the tiny Le Pin are all excellent and expensive.

Pomerol wine is all red, made mostly from Merlot, and they differ from St-Emilions in their added richness and, in good years, complexity. The area is small, production modest and fame great — so there is little 'ordinary' Pomerol. These are not wines to age for decades, though Pétrus can last a lifetime. It is perhaps one clue to their popularity that even the top wines taste good while still young: millionaires want their fun now.

THE OTHER LIBOURNAIS WINES

Libourne grew up as a port, the outlet for the wines of its hinterland which became known as the Libournais.

For centuries, there were no bridges across the wide rivers that divide the St-Emilion country from the city of Bordeaux. For much of this period, politics as well as geography split the Libournais from Bordeaux. The trade of Libourne took the wines of Pomerol and St-Emilion to a wider world, and drew on the back-country too: Fronsac just next door to the west, the villages of St-Georges, Lussac and their neighbours to the northeast. Bustling Libourne still has many wine firms today.

These once minor wines are now sought for, as cheaper alternatives to the well-known names. Some, such as Montagne, St-Georges and Lussac, can by law add St-Emilion to their names. This stresses their common character. Fronsac and Canon-Fronsac have more in common with Pomerol — perhaps because the same people own many of the best vineyards. Over to the east, the Côtes de Castillon and Côtes de Francs have emerged from the obscurity of the basic Bordeaux appellation only recently.

All these places make satisfying red wines which can be enjoyed quite young. Some aspire to age in bottle, but they are rarely to be kept beyond five or six years.

Château Ausone, one of the two top estates of St-Emilion, is perched on the edge of the limestone slope known as 'the côte'. This slope provides good drainage and a sunny site for the vines.

THE REST OF BORDEAUX

On thousands of small farms across the Gironde département, people grow grapes and (sometimes) make wine without more than a wry glance at the elegant châteaux of the Médoc, or the ancient glories of St-Emilion. Wine here is a crop, with its annual ups and downs of yield, price and accident. The label on the bottle says AOC Bordeaux, with perhaps a château name, or more likely that of a négociant (merchant) who buys the wine and blends it.

This basic bordeaux — perhaps called claret if red (and exported), perhaps labelled Bordeaux Sauvignon if white — is one of the staple drinks of France and is enjoyed around the world. Within the region some areas have special names for certain types of wine:

Entre-Deux-Mers, the wide land between the 'seas' or rivers of the Dordogne and the Garonne, is a white-wine name. Here innumerable properties make white wine and call it Entre-Deux-Mers, and red wine and call it straightforward AOC Bordeaux. Many of the farms here grow wine as one of

a range of crops. There are fewer specialist estates than in the classic areas. Cooperatives process much of the fruit, making the wine and either selling it in bulk or returning it, bottled, to the grower. The best of these cooperatives, and a sprinkling of private estates, have brought modern white-wine techniques to the Entre-Deux-Mers. What was a byword for boring white wine can now be the signal for fresh, tasty bottles which combine crispness with full fruit.

On the slopes above the Garonne, the Premières Côtes de Bordeaux vineyards are heirs to medieval reputations now eclipsed by those of Graves on the opposite bank. They still make supple, interesting red wines, mostly from Merlot. Further south, opposite Sauternes, a few villages such as Loupiac and St-Croix-du-Mont persevere with sweet white wines which merchants puzzle to sell.

Across the wide Gironde from the Médoc lie the hilly vineyards of Blaye. With those of Bourg to the south-east, they were making good red wine when the Médoc was so much marshland. Since this medieval heyday other wines have improved, but the virtues of Bourg and Blaye remain. Some whites are made here, but the reds are the best.

Few of the *petits châteaux* of Bordeaux have a discoverable local identity, short of some hard work on the small-print of the address. This does not matter: the job of the merchants is to search out good-value wines, irrespective of area, and the wide vineyards of Bordeaux give them plenty of scope. It is hard to see red bordeaux at the ordinary level getting too expensive, but it faces increasing competition from other places — not least from its old rivals inland beyond the Gironde department frontier.

VINTAGES

The different grape varieties, and climates, of the various Bordeaux regions, make vintage judgments for the entire region hard to reach. The claret connoisseur learns quickly that a good Médoc vintage can be a St-Emilion disaster, a fine year in Pauillac can be a poor one in Margaux. The sweet wines of Sauternes, just to be difficult, rarely follow the 'good' years of red bordeaux.

Rose bushes are traditionally planted at the ends of rows of vines in Bordeaux — not just for decoration, but to warn of the approach of diseases such as mildew, which the rose bush will get first.

SOUTH-WEST FRANCE

Travel east and south-east from Bordeaux, following the broad valleys of the Dordogne and Garonne into the ancient province of Gascony, and the vines keep you company; not constantly, but in considerable patches. They only cease where the rivers run through the high gorges of the Massif Central or the foothills of the Pyrenees.

These are the vineyards of South-west France — what the medieval Bordeaux merchants called the Haut-Pays: 'the up-country'. This somewhat derogatory term gives a clue to the rivalry between the Bordeaux trade and the growers of Gaillac, Cahors, Fronton and the other areas upstream. Bordeaux took advantage of its waterfront position to keep these wines out of the export markets. Each year, ships were banned from taking these wines to England and elsewhere in northern Europe until the Bordeaux wines had been successfully shipped. This ban, based upon force but later codified into law (the so-called '*privilège de Bordeaux*') turned these vineyards into backwaters.

Now the wines come to market by road, they can live on their merits. Many areas are reviving after a century of decline. Numerous holidaymakers visit the beautiful valleys of the Tarn, Lot and Dordogne — and take home a taste for Gaillac, Cahors and Bergerac.

The wines of the Dordogne begin with Bergerac, a wide appellation which begins where the Bordeaux zones of Côtes de Franc and St-Foy-Bordeaux end. Indeed, the Montravel sub-zone of Bergerac faces St-Foy across the river. The wines are bordeaux in taste if not name: good-value reds from Cabernet and Merlot grapes, whites from Sauvignon Blanc and Sémillon. The heart of Bergerac is the sub-zone of Monbazillac, where fine sweet whites are made. Many of the best reds carry the name of the favoured, hilly Pécharmant district.

Move on south, through the beautiful rolling country of Gascony, and you reach the Duras vineyards beneath their splendid castle, one of many reminders that this was a frontier between the English-owned part of France and that controlled by the French crown. The Marmandais vineyard slopes down to the Garonne. These two districts both make attractive Bordeaux-style red wines, and Duras makes good, crisp whites for drinking young.

Follow the Garonne valley upstream and you tread one of the great highways of the ancient and medieval worlds,

Many towers and castles survive from the days when this was a frontier region.

the road that linked the Mediterranean and the Atlantic at Bordeaux. Wine flowed down this river in Roman times, bound for Britain. Buzet is the first modern vineyard, with mostly red wines. Then away to the south come the rich lands of Armagnac, where grapes are grown for brandy — and, increasingly, for good-value white wine under the name Vins de Pays des Côtes de Gascogne. Toulouse gets a good supply of soft, red wine from the Côtes du Frontonnais.

Away to the east, around the Tarn Valley, the vineyards of Gaillac yield a variety of wines: white and red, even sparkling. All are designed for drinking young. Here are found grapes unknown in Bordeaux, dating from Roman days when Gaillac had vines but Bordeaux did not.

Cahors makes red wines that aspire to higher quality than most in the South-west. The zone's personality is stressed by its ban on Bordeaux's Cabernet vines: the wine must be mostly Auxerrois (called Malbec in Bordeaux). There are two different styles of Cahors: some wines, from top estates, are tough and need ageing, others are softer and mature more quickly.

Down in the far south, where the Pyrenees shelter the unique Basque culture, are found a flock of wines with strange names and delicious tastes. Madiran, a characterful and long-ageing red, is the best-known. Others are mostly drunk where they are made, though the occasional bottle of honey-sweet Jurançon finds its way out to delight wine-lovers.

THE LOIRE VALLEY

The River Loire, all 1020km (634 miles) of it, uncurls itself across the heart of France. Its mild, rich, smiling farmlands were close enough to Paris for kings and courtiers to build hunting lodges, châteaux and palaces on the river banks. Its vineyards have never achieved the fame of its palaces: uncertain northern weather makes for unpredictable vintages, and Paris was traditionally served by Champagne, Burgundy and other vineyards upstream. The Loire's markets were thus, like Bordeaux's, overseas. Dutch buyers wanted thin white wine for distilling — and that is what they got. A few pockets of quality developed: Chinon has had a name for red wine for centuries, Anjou's sweet wines had a reputation. Other wines now well (indeed, internationally) known, such as Muscadet, Sancerre and Pouilly Fumé, had purely local fame a few decades ago.

The Loire is still the hunting ground for the lover of the

The village of Sancerre stands on a vine-clad hill above the upper Loire.

unknown, local wine, Thousands of growers make wine, many selling it only to direct buyers and local restaurants. Here the traveller will find wines whose tiny production means that, however well-made, they never make their way to the wine store shelves or the fashionable wine lists. Conversely, some Loire merchant firms sell uninspiring wines that cling to the name of a famous appellation without offering much of its true character.

Start near the sea, where Nantes has its own wine in the dry, white Muscadet. Sadly, much bad Muscadet, harsh and acidic, is made and sold both in France and abroad. The real thing is soft yet bone dry, with enough tangy flavour and character to partner seafood. Look for individual estate wines, and for those labelled *sur lie*: these, bottled without racking, have an extra complexity of taste.

This western end of the valley makes quite a few other wines, mostly white. The *vin de pays* name for this whole region, Jardin de la France, can be found on a large range of wines. Some growers use it for novelties like Chardonnay whites, or Cabernet Franc reds, grown outside their usual haunts. Worth a trial if you are feeling adventurous.

The other appellations of western Loire are best avoided unless you find, by trial and error, a grower to trust. Gros Plant is usually hard, acidic and pointless when Muscadet costs little more. Coteaux d'Ancienis reds are rarely a match for those made up-river, such as Anjou and Chinon.

If the ocean end of the valley is the place to look for crisp whites but not much more, the middle reaches get more interesting — and more complex. Angers, with its great squat castle, is the capital of Anjou. Here are made wines of every sort: plenty of rosé, whites dry and sweet, and increasing amounts of red. The map of appellations here is a confusing muddle. Look for a few key names, avoid a few others, and the groundwork is done. Anjou Rosé, labelled as such and/or as Rosé d'Anjou, is rarely worth a corkscrew. Cabernet d'Anjou is a better bet: the Cabernet grapes bring some flavour and character. Rosé de Loire, if you come across it, is supposed to be drier than Anjou Rosé.

Red wines used to be rare in Anjou, but more are appearing. Try Anjou Rouge — especially if labelled Anjou Villages, which comes from the best area south-east of Angers.

The real glory of Anjou is its sweet white wine. The Layon, a little river that joins the Loire west of Anjou, provides a

Harvesting at Reuilly in the upper Loire vineyards.

valley with ideal conditions for noble rot (see Sauternes page 46). Not every year works the magic, but when the autumn mists linger some wonderful wines can be made. The grape is Chenin Blanc, which in its dry form can taste of little, but which can age into delightful, complex, nutty sweetness. Good dry wines are made here too, but for reliability stick to the star names like Savennières, which are not expensive for their quality, rather than basic Anjou Blanc.

Saumur, upstream, shelters a thriving sparkling-wine industry which ages its millions of bottles in caves cut from the limestone rock. Sparkling Saumur has improved recently as grapes such as Chardonnay have been added to the blend. It is worth paying a little more for a luxury *cuvée*: the standard stuff can have plenty of fizz but little flavour. Saumur also makes pleasant red wine from the Cabernet Franc grape. The best name is Saumur-Champigny: wine from the heart of the area. It can be delicious, and is very fashionable in Paris as a lunch-time wine, especially with fish.

On past Saumur the valley winds into the province of Touraine, with castles and ancient villages crowning every vista. Chinon's castle, which guards a bridge over the River Vienne, rivals Saumur's. It gives its name to a red wine which can be among the most delicious and fascinating in France. The grape is Cabernet Franc. Look out for the estate name here: as in much of the Loire, there is a contrast between carefully-crafted single-domaine wines and those from the big merchant houses. Chinon from a good vintage — one with enough summer sun, which happens about three years in ten — can age in bottle for a decade. Normally, drink it slightly chilled at two to four years old. Bourgeuil, across the Loire to the north, makes very similar wine.

Touraine offers great white wines from Vouvray and nearby Montlouis. The Chenin Blanc grape plays the same tricks as in Anjou: dry and harsh in poor years, honeyed and delightful in warm ones. The problem with Vouvray is to work out which is which. Short of consulting a detailed vintage report, it is hard to know whether a bottle contains sweet wine or dry. Look for estate wines, avoid merchants' ones, and remember the label terms: *molleaux* means sweet, *demi-sec* medium-dry and *sec*, dry. *Molleaux* wines are rare: a really warm autumn is necessary, and that can happen but once in a decade. *Demi-sec* Vouvray from a good grower can be a tasty and tantalising balance of sweetness and acidity: delicious when young, superb with age. Dry Vouvray is harder to characterise: buy from growers with a reputation. Vouvray can age for decades, and in doing so the *demi-sec* wines acquire superb flavours. These are not really wines for meal-times, but (like Germany's Mosels) drinks for a warm summer evening or a winter fireside.

The Loire's vineyards end with a flourish around Sancerre and Pouilly. Here are made two of the most popular white wines in the world, Sancerre and Pouilly-Fumé. Not so long ago, hardly a restaurant failed to list them, and Sancerre was the best-selling wine in more than one smart London brasserie. Now, New World competitors such as New Zealand Sauvignon have stolen some of the market. A welcome wave of common sense has washed over the twin appellation. Prices are down, quality is improving. Both wines are made from Sauvignon Blanc, which on the chalk soil here shows a tense, sparky character. A good example has fruit to go with the acidity, and an appetising smell of green grass and gooseberries. Poor wines are merely acidic and pungent. It is a good taster who can tell Pouilly from Sancerre, but most can tell Pouilly Fumé, which does seem to have a whiff of smoke in its makeup, from Pouilly-sur-

Loire: a lesser wine, softer and flatter, made from a different grape. There is a little red wine in Sancerre, but it usually lacks both colour and conviction and the prices are as high as those of the much more reliable Chinons.

Other vineyards dot the countryside all the way to the mountains where the Loire has its source. Mainly local wines, to be enjoyed locally. Try Menetou-Salon and Quincy if you spot them: good Sancerre-like wines at lower prices.

The main Loire vineyards are flanked by dozens of minor zones which hardly ever achieve wide fame. Some have recently planted grapes untypical of the Loire and these make wines out of the normal run. Those that might be encountered outside their home county include the wines of Haut-Poitou, to the south of the main valley. Here Sauvignon and Chardonnay whites, and reds and rosés from Gamay and Cabernet, find buyers at attractive prices. Valençay, also to the south, is a little-known district making some good red and rosé wines from Cabernet and Gamay. Cheverny, a little further north, makes good white wines from the traditional Chenin Blanc and Sauvignon, to which enterprising growers have added some Chardonnay. There are also red wines.

Houses on this hillside at Vouvray extend backwards into the soft tufa rock of the hillside, forming wine caves which burrow beneath the great 15th century château of Moncontour.

BURGUNDY, CHAMPAGNE & THE EAST

THE EASTERN SIDE OF FRANCE is at first glance a big area to generalise about, but in wine terms there are strong strands of taste and history that make the parallels possible. There is a real difference in style between the wines of western and eastern France. These come from the grapes used, the climate and some accidents of history. Burgundy is the heart of the eastern side, as Bordeaux is of the west. Burgundy's great grape varieties, Pinot Noir for red wines and Chardonnay for whites, are also used in Champagne to the north, in the Jura on the Swiss frontier and even (in the case of Pinot Noir and its white cousins) in faraway Alsace on the German border.

The climate here is harsher than in the west. No soft sea breezes blow in to moderate summer heat or winter chill. Snow lies on the bleak ridges of Champagne and tops the Beaujolais

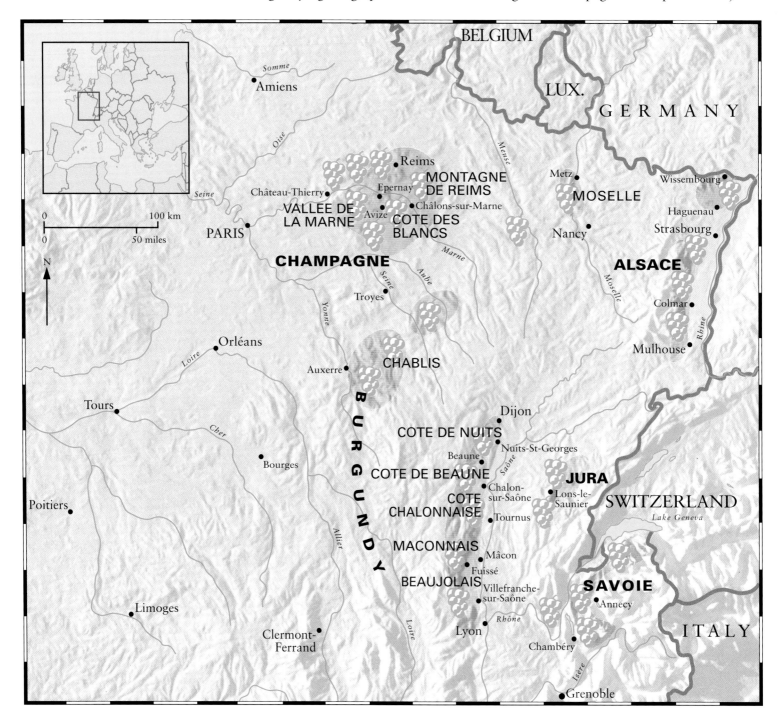

*M. Gaston Mignot is in charge of the
Romanée-Conti estate's vines in the
famous Le Montrachet Grand Cru
vineyard. The reeds are for tying vines to
their stakes.*

*The precious vines of the Côte d'Or form
a priceless pattern, here at Auxey-
Duresses.*

The Meursault vineyard of Les Genevrières, a Premier Cru, falls away to the east.

hills. The Alps and the Jura mountains rise on eastern horizons.

History, too, has made its contribution. When Bordeaux was English, and the wine fleet bore away thousands of casks every autumn, Burgundy and Champagne were sending theirs to Paris. The pattern has remained intact. Even today, it is easier in Paris to find good burgundy than good bordeaux.

THE CÔTE D'OR

Bourgogne (Burgundy is the English name) is an ancient province of France. Its princes once rivalled the kings in Paris. Its wealth is evident still in great buildings, and in a taste for opulence in eating and drinking. The feasts of Burgundy are famous. So are the vineyards, with names that have resonance everywhere wine is drunk: Romanée-Conti, Pommard, Chassagne-Montrachet, Chablis, Gevry-Chambertin.

The heart of the scattered burgundian vineyard is the strip of hills called the Côte d'Or — the 'golden slope'. These low hills face east and south-east, and are sheltered from west and north by a broad band of upland forest. There are other such favoured slopes in central France, but no other has Dijon, ancient capital of Burgundy, beside it. Nor do other slopes have the great road from Paris to the South at their feet.

The rock that makes these hills has its contribution to make to the mix formed from aspect, microclimate and history. The grape varieties seem to suit the conditions to perfection. Together all these ingredients made the names of Nuits-St-George, Chambertin, Beaune, a thousand years ago.

The puzzle for modern winelovers is to sort out the present reality from the myths of past glory. It is little help to learn that Napoleon drank Chambertin, or that the monks made Vougeout famous. What do they taste like now, and which ones are the best? The second question is hardest to answer. For every one great château over in the Médoc, there are twenty, perhaps sixty, names to memorise here in the Côte d'Or. Unlike the self-contained Bordeaux estates, here the famous vineyards are in multiple ownership. Each vineyard is a tangle of tiny plots. Each grower owns plots in several vineyards. Each merchant buys from a dozen, a score, a hundred growers. Maybe he blends the wines, maybe they keep their identities. Add the fickle Burgundy climate, and thus variable vintages, and it is enough to drive the impatient back to the certainties of New World wines, or the comparative sanity of Bordeaux.

Some details cannot be avoided. First, the hierarchy. The Côte d'Or expresses all the good and bad points about the

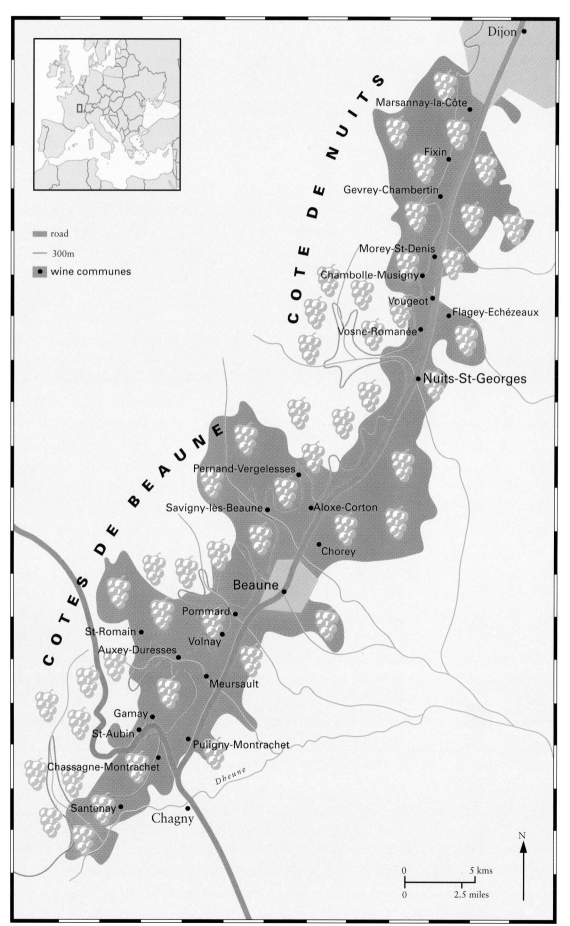

Wine for sale: bottles of Beaune Premier Cru on display at the Château de Meursault.

The Côte d'Or, with its string of famous wine villages.

French appellation system. There are four ranks of wine, these being (from lowest to highest) regional, village, *premier cru* and *grand cru*. The higher the rank the smaller the area of vineyard which can claim it, down to the few acres of the *grands crus*.

It is tempting to think that a *premier cru* wine will always be better than a village wine. It should be, but the human factor intervenes. A clever winemaker can make more of a village wine than a slapdash one will of a *premier cru*. So there are two names to watch for on the label: the place, or vineyard, and the maker.

The picture is clearer for white burgundy, so we will deal with that to get started. The greatest names — Montrachet, for instance — are wines for millionaires. There are no more pricy whites, except perhaps Yquem. Forget *grands crus*, then, and look for value among the *premiers crus* and the village wines. Chardonnay is more robust and reliable than Pinot Noir, so white wines have a higher success rate. Most of the white vineyards are in the southern half of the Côte d'Or, the Côte de Beaune. Here are found Meursault, with its powerful wines that age well. Puligny and Chassagne are twin villages that share the wonderful Montrachet *grand cru* and thus attach themselves to its name. The lesser wines of both are a touch more elegant than Meursaults.

In general, Côte d'Or whites are serious wines for solemn occasions. Other areas (Chablis, Chalonnais, Mâcon) make more light-hearted wines for shorter pockets.

Red burgundy, in its Côte d'Or versions, is one of the hardest of great wines to describe and one of the easiest to enjoy. Once they have shed the edgy, tannic taste that oak casks confer, they are silky, fruity and perfumed, with a long-lasting flavour. The many villages of the Côte each add their subtleties, simply expressed as a greater or lesser degree of weight. No red burgundy, by the way, should be truly heavy. The days of the bogus blended burgundies which owed much to southern French wines are long gone, but the myth lingers.

Working down from Dijon in the north, the most famous red burgundies come from Gevrey-Chambertin — fruity and well-structured; Morey St-Denis: long-lived and solid; Chambolle-Musigny: more grace yet with power; Clos de Vougeot: rich, heady; Vosne-Romanée: opulent, silky; Nuits-St-George: full and robust. Within this roll-call are other vineyards, not attached to villages but with solitary names of their own. Chambertin, La Romanée, Richebourg and the like are *grands crus*. This rank will not appear on the label, just the name. The idea seems to be that if you can afford such wines, you can remember their names. Beware the trap of thinking that a wine from a village which shares a *grand cru* name (for example Chambolle-Musigny) is a *grand cru*. Ordinary 'village' wine will carry the words Chambolle-Musigny AOC. A wine ranking as a *premier cru*, the grade below *grand*, will say so on the label.

Affordable red burgundy can be found in the Côte d'Or. Look for wines with the village AOCs, labelled just plain Pommard or Volnay, for example, or with Côtes de Nuits-Villages or Côtes de Beaune-Villages on the label: these wines come from small villages without the status to sell under their own names.

When seeking such wines, the name of the producer matters most. There are two kinds: négociants and growers. The former buy and blend wine, the latter both grow the grapes and make the wines. There is of course much overlap: négociants may own vineyards too. Reputations vary from dire to delicious, and they can change fast. Take note of the people behind the wine as well as the place, and buy accordingly. Good advice can be had from wine merchants who work daily with the complexities of Burgundy, but names cannot sensibly be given here.

CHABLIS

Life is simpler in Chablis. All the wine is white, from Chardonnay of course; and it is a fair bet that the *grands crus* will taste better than the *premiers*. There are rather too many *premier cru* vineyards for the standard to be quite as high as it ought to be, but some excellent growers are riding the crest of the Chardonnay wave to make and sell good, flavoursome wine.

Chablis is described in old books as very dry. So it was; but much today is made in a softer, almost fruity-sweet style. Chablis-lovers say these wines will age into something more akin to the classic, austere style, but some seem to do little maturing, merely staying rather flabby.

Despite the changes in style, Chablis remains a good bet, though 'bet' is the word as the taste can vary quite widely depending upon maker and vintage. Being far north, Chablis can suffer from cold, wet summers and frosty springs. Try to taste a few Chablis, and when you find a reliable source, stick

Vines lap right up to the walls of the houses in the Burgundian village of Meursault. The flat land away in the distance is not used for vines.

to it. As with all burgundian wines, handle restaurant Chablis with care unless the list proudly states its provenance. Some négociants cannot resist the temptation to bottle bland and unhappy wines knowing that the Chablis name will carry them past uncritical buyers.

SOUTHERN BURGUNDY

South of the Côte d'Or the wine maps show several distinct areas: the Côte Chalonnais, Mâconnais, Beaujolais. On the ground, amid the woods and streams of this beautiful countryside, boundaries are hard to spot. The southern end of the Côte d'Or is the last organised bit of landscape: the bold ridge breaks here into a tangle of hills. Wine villages dot the area, amid more general farms. Most grow the Pinot Noir for red burgundy, and the Chardonnay for white. They use the names of their villages or those of the general Burgundy appellations: variations on the name Bourgogne. The exception is Beaujolais, where the somewhat steeper hills grow Gamay vines for red wine which is distinct in character.

Wine labelled AOC Bourgogne, sometimes with the grape name, can come from anywhere in this zone. The best reds are from Mercurey and Rully in the Chalonnais. Ordinary Mâcon red is adequate. Whites are most famous from Pouilly-Fuissé (not to be confused with Pouilly-Fumé from the Loire); best value from Montagny, Rully or labelled as Mâcon-Villages. Much of the wine from around here is made by cooperatives, which can reach quite high standards and offer good value. Look out for their oak-aged examples, labelled '*fût de chêne*'.

Beaujolais, like Chablis, is sold too much on its famous name and not enough on its flavour. When good, usually bought direct from the grower, it can be deliciously light, heady and fruity. Many examples are heavy, over-sweet and flabby. The most prestigious and flavoursome Beaujolais comes from the 10 'Crus' — villages allowed to use their own name on the label. Morgon and Fleurie are the best-known.

CHAMPAGNE

The dour streets of Reims and Epernay have little frivolity about them. Yet beneath your feet, and behind the grey stone walls, are millions of bottles of the wine of celebration: champagne. The fizz that has launched untold thousands of ships, parties and weddings ought by rights to come from somewhere jolly and southern. But the mix of cool vineyards and canny cellar technique combines perfectly here in northern France to make the inimitable best sparkling wine of all.

Champagne the land is one of the ancient provinces of France. Its rolling wheat fields and forests are crossed by two of the great roads of Europe, that from Germany to Paris and the north-south route from Flanders to the South. The crossroads meant, in medieval times, a trade fair. These fairs, plus the monasteries that early on established themselves in Champagne, meant a market for wine. The monks, and increasingly the laity, planted vines to make a wine that was in demand by kings and courtiers. This wine was red, and still. The bubbles came later, as did the perfection of cellar techniques that allowed white wine to be made from black

grapes. As late as the time of Napoleon, only one bottle of champagne in ten was fizzy. The habit of linking sparkling champagne to celebration was well established. But the process was hard to perfect: bottles burst, wine was wasted and cellar-workers lived dangerous lives.

Why the fizz? Champagne's late harvests and cool cellars often means that new wine does not quite finish fermenting before the winter cold stops the yeasts working. Spring warmth starts the process off again. If the wine is bottled over the winter, then the renewed fermentation causes bubbles in the wine. Take off the cork, and the result is fizz as the carbon dioxide bubbles escape.

Today, this second fermentation is a managed affair, not an accident. The wine is made as normal, the only unusual detail being Champagne's use of black Pinot Noir and Pinot Meunier grapes to make white wine. This demands careful, gentle pressing to extract the (colourless) juice — but not the tint that comes from the black grape skins.

Once the wine is made, it is blended. Each firm has its 'recipe'. Wines from the various grape varieties and vineyard areas will be blended, sometimes with reserve wines from earlier years. Then the wine is bottled, with the addition of a small dose of yeast mixed with wine and sugar to trigger the second fermentation. The second fermentation takes place inside the bottle, and the tightly-corked bottles rest in the endless cellars for up to two years. Then the residue of fermentation — mostly dead yeast cells — must be disgorged. To enable this to happen the bottles are stored neck down and gently turned to nudge the sediment into the neck. This process, known as *remuage*, was once done by hand, but is now increasingly mechanised. The bottle necks are frozen, uncorked and the 'plug' extracted. Now the champagne is corked (with the proper wired cork), labelled and ready. Perfectionist makers keep the wine a little longer to let it mature a little more.

So much for the method. It can be, and is, used elsewhere: look for the term 'bottle-fermented' on wines from most quality wine zones. Many are excellent, but none taste quite like champagne. Why do the Champagne vineyards make such good raw materials? The right grapes, on the right soil,

Champagne is about cellarwork as much as growing grapes: here the position of the sediment in a bottle of Perrier-Jouet 'Belle Epoque' rosé is carefully checked.

in the right place is the answer. Chardonnay, as grown for white Burgundy, is the one white grape; while Pinot Noir and Pinot Meunier are the black ones. Soils in the area vary: the best sites are on chalk, which appears in a deep band along the aptly-named Côte des Blancs (white soil and white grapes) south of Epernay, and along the edge of the forested hills of the Montagne de Reims. These are the best areas, though there are six others.

The best champagne comes from these top vineyard areas, and from makers who can afford to blend their wine from a wide palate and age it to maturity. These makers are the champagne firms, which both own vineyards and make the wine. Other vineyard-owners sell their grapes or new wine to these firms, while some of these small-scale growers make their own champagne. These 'grower' champagnes are cheaper than the great names (the '*Grandes Marques*') but on the whole they offer less complexity and character.

Champagne turns one wine convention on its head. Here, the best wines are not those from the smallest, most strictly defined vineyards and the most perfect years. Champagne is a blend of wines and vintages. There are *grand cru* vineyards, but few wines from them appear unblended. Most champagne is

The vineyard slopes of Verzenay on the Montagne de Reims are crowned by a picturesque windmill.

thus non-vintage, while a few bottles carry a date. Champagne makers proclaim their habit of blending from different years as a virtue, for it evens out quality troughs and ensures consistency. This consistency is by no means always apparent, and many wine lovers feel that the extra depth of taste of a vintage wine is worth the small amount more they cost.

Vintage wines need time in bottle to mature to their best, but even non-vintage champagnes can improve with some bottle-age. Try to keep your champagne for a year, and taste the difference.

Pink or rosé champagne has a wonderfully decadent image. Some taste as good as they look, but others are anaemic in every sense. The occasional still wines of Champagne, both white and red, are a curiosity (reminders of what champagne used to be like) and a treat with the often excellent cuisine of the region.

Next two pages: Krug Grande Cuvée champagne rests in pupitres in the chalk caves deep beneath the city of Reims.

ALSACE

Somewhere between Champagne and Alsace, going east, you cross an unmarked gastronomic frontier. The flavour becomes Central European rather than French: food, wine and scenery — hearty, savoury meals, cool white wine and dark forested hills — conspire to change the atmosphere.

History and geography have linked the wines of Alsace to Germany rather than France. The Rhine, which now forms the frontier, has been a trade route as much as a barrier. Alsace wines once took their place on the shipping lists of the Rhine merchants alongside their German counterparts. The greatest Alsace grapes, Riesling and Gewürztraminer, are German in origin, as is Sylvaner; though Alsace also grows the French-accented Pinots Blanc and Noir, and Pinot Gris which is a cousin.

To add to the paradox, however, nearly all Alsace wine, while sharing the flowery fruit of the best German, is truly French in style: dry, crisp and appetizing. These are meal-time bottles, not wines for sipping alone as are most Germans. And Alsace wine is easy to understand: it is nearly all white, the grape name is large and clear on the label, the few exceptions to the 'Alsace means dry' rule are clearly signalled. (They are *vendange tardive* wines — late-picked — and *sélection des grains nobles*: from selected grapes *á la* Sauternes.)

Riesling is the wine the Alsatians are proudest of. In contrast to most German examples, Alsace Rieslings are dry, full-flavoured and aromatic, while subtle. They can age well, showing the lovely lemony fruit and richness of the grape at about five years old.

Gewürztraminer, by contrast, makes very loud wine. It is fruity, spicy and unmistakable, and can be delicious. Not a wine to drink every day, but fun on its own and a good partner to rich food.

Pinot Gris has more class. It is solid and full, with some of the character of white Burgundy. Pinot Blanc makes sharper, lighter wine. Gris for mealtimes, Blanc beforehand.

You will also find (dry) Muscats, the occasional pale red from Pinot Noir, and sparkling wine called Crémant d'Alsace which can be very good value.

Most Alsace wines are sold according to grape names and the names of the makers, but there is a list of individual vineyard sites, the *grands crus*. These have been picked as the best spots to grow specific grape varieties, mostly Riesling. *Grand cru* wines can be expected to be more intensely flavoured and to be capable of ageing. They are expensive, but they represent the best of Alsace winemaking.

Most Alsace wine is made by merchant houses which buy grapes and wine from growers. Few estates exist, in the sense found in other parts of France. The local cooperatives are a major force in Alsace and make some very good wines.

JURA AND SAVOIE

Alsace is not the only frontier vineyard. Jura and Savoie also stand isolated in the east of France. The Jura vineyards, amid the mountains of the same name, are not far from Burgundy, on the road to Switzerland. The Savoie districts lie further south, across the upper Rhône, tucked into corners of the beautiful sub-Alpine valleys east of Lyons.

Neither district makes much wine for export, though their specialities are much appreciated locally and by tourists. The Jura is perhaps the more sophisticated of the two, with a good range of wines of every colour. The reds, from the Pinot Noir grape of Burgundy plus some local varieties, are attractive. Whites, from Chardonnay and local grapes, are fresh and delicate. The local speciality is *vin jaune*, a wine whose closest cousin is the faraway fino sherry of southern Spain. *Vin jaune* is allowed to oxidise during its long maturation, creating a nutty flavour. This is a wine for quiet reflective moments, not for mealtimes.

Savoie makes red and white wines, of which the whites are the best. They are made to be drunk young and cool. Red wines from the Mondeuse grape are a local speciality. The wine is dark, full-flavoured and distinctly old-fashioned, but it is rare. Sparkling wines are also made in Savoie but they, like much of the rest of the production, are mostly drunk in the region by tourists.

THE SOUTH

FRANCE HAS ANOTHER unmarked frontier, that between north and south. In the Rhône Valley south of Lyons you pass into the Mediterranean world, with vines as the natural crop instead of a speciality for warm corners. Here is found a new repertoire of grape varieties and wine styles. The whole of southern France, from the northern Rhône right down to the Italian and Spanish frontiers, has a common identity. The red wines are warm, scented and (at their best) dense and spicy. The whites are full and tend to be flabby: this is not the place to look for fresh, crisp wines. The range of quality is very broad: some wines, from the northern Rhône and Châteauneuf-du-Pape, rival the greatest reds of Bordeaux and Burgundy. Much of the rest is only just above bulk wine status. The South does have a sense of excitement

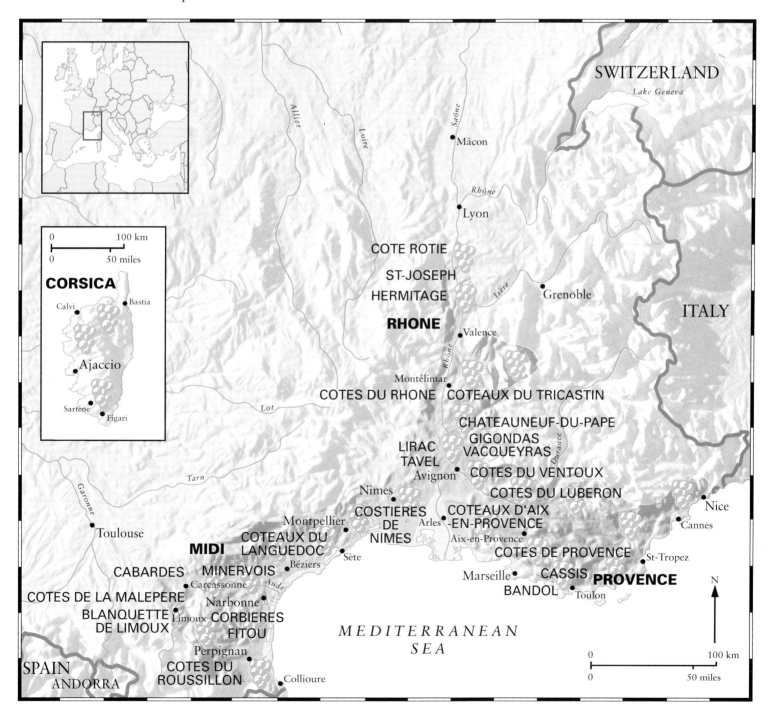

about it: here, the potential exists for great wines to be discovered, sometimes rediscovered. In the classic zones further north, the stars are already on the official lists.

THE RHÔNE

The Rhône vineyards begin near Vienne, where the hills above the river are cool and northern but the favoured valley slopes catch the increasingly southern sun. Hereabouts are made robust red wines that are increasingly prized by connoisseurs. Luckily there is also a range of good-value reds which offer flavour and character.

The Côte Rôtie — the sun-soaked 'roasted hill' towering above the river — makes superb, long-lived wines; but in tiny amounts. Hermitage and Cornas are similarly small and much in demand. Hermitage is the senior wine of the Rhône,

with the capacity to age for decades. It was once as expensive as the great Bordeaux reds and the price is again climbing. Look for similar flavours, and easier prices, from St-Joseph and Crozes-Hermitage. The common thread of all these wines is the Syrah grape. When made well, this is dark, spicy, tannic wine that can age into a subtle, scented masterpiece. Do not expect all this from mid-priced Crozes, but do look forward to a decent mouthful for the money.

Further south, the vines take to the plains and the yield is enormous. Here are found the straightforward Côtes du Rhône vineyards, source of much supermarket wine, bought by French families without much thought. The occasional

The chapel on the crest of the great hill of Hermitage gives its name to the La Chapelle vineyard. Beyond are Tain l'Hermitage and the Rhône.

good red emerges, but there are other names that promise far more flavour for your money. Look for the word '–Villages' tacked onto Côtes du Rhône: these wines are from the top villages. Some places proudly use their own names: Gigondas and Vacqueyras lead the rest. Most of this wine is red, with dark hues, spicy scents and a capacity to age in bottle: two years old for a '–Villages', four to eight for the best wines.

The reds of the southern Rhône are made from a wide range of grapes. Some of the good ones use Syrah, the grape of the northern Rhône, but usually as a minority component to add flavour. Mourvèdre, a fascinating red grape from Provence, is also used in a similar role. Most ordinary Côtes du Rhône reds will be made from Grenache.

White wines are less successful in this hot country. Some white Hermitage is made, using Marsanne and Roussanne vines. The growers of Condrieu use the Viognier grape, newly fashionable in California and Australia, to make a luscious white that tastes of peaches. Some white Côtes du Rhône is produced, but most is less than exciting. White Châteauneuf is more interesting.

Châteauneuf-du-Pape is one of those wines whose name is so well-known that it is the typeface on the label which sells. Much is disappointing, rather like Chablis, because restaurants of the un-adventurous sort feel they have to have a Châteauneuf, and merchants are happy to provide it. No-one worries much about the taste. A few great estates make superb wine here: know them by their prices, which though high are not exorbitant for the quality. The grapes are a wide-ranging blend: some estates use 13 varieties. Good red Châteauneuf needs six years in bottle, the white less.

THE MIDI

As the Rhône valley widens the vineyards become virtually continuous. A great belt runs east and west from the river's delta, taking in Provence to the east and the Languedoc to the west. Hardly a village here, in a great swathe of country between sea to the south and mountains to the north, is without vines.

There is plenty of wine to be had here, but sorting out the good from the downright dire is a full-time job. Luckily, the world's wine merchants are realising that this tract is a source of good everyday wine — and the occasional star. The habit of the Midi, as the French sometimes call this land, has been to

The idyllic vineyard country of the Côte d'Azur, where Côtes de Provence wine is made within sight of the Mediterranean.

make too much wine, too badly. There is no market for mass-produced red any more, so the search is on for flavours that will entice the palates of the modern winelover.

The best wines are red, though the incursions of Australian winemakers have proved that Chardonnay can be grown here to good effect. A bewildering number of influences plays on the region. Old-established grape varieties, and vines, contribute rustic flavours; classic vines such as Cabernet, Merlot and Syrah add cosmopolitan notes. The real change comes from improved techniques in vineyard and winery. Low prices and conservatism had trapped the Midi in the past, using the methods of a century ago at a time when other regions were seizing on the latest ideas. Now there are enough modern wineries, both private and run by cooperatives, to point the way forward — and the results can be tasted.

The names to look for include a clutch of appellations: Minervois, Corbières and Côtes-du-Roussillon-Villages. All these are hilly zones with good sites for red wine. Formerly,

Fields of lavender amid the vines in the Midi.

statements such as '*fûts de chêne*' stressing oak-ageing. This is the land of experiment — and not all experiments work; but the chance of an exciting red wine at a good price is higher here than anywhere else in France.

The search for good white wine is harder. Some *vins de pays* use Chardonnay and Sauvignon grapes to good effect. The enclave of Limoux in the hills close to Spain makes fine sparkling wine and increasing amounts of useful still whites.

A speciality of the Midi, in particular the southwest corner, the ancient province of Roussillon, is sweet fortified wine. These wines are confusingly called *vins doux naturels*. Sweet (*doux*) they usually are, but hardly natural in the sense in which the term is usually used for wine, as they are fortified with brandy. These wines date right back to the discover of distillation, credited (in Europe at least) to a scholar at Montpellier 800 years ago. The dose of brandy stops the wine's fermentation, leaving some natural sweetness. These are wines for sipping after dinner, or on a warm evening, though the French enjoy them as apéritifs. Banyuls and Rivesaltes are the best appellations, while others from Muscat grapes (the word will be on the label) add a fresh grapey note to the sweetness.

the wine was made by cooperatives and sold anonymously. Now, estate names increasingly feature on labels as newcomers from Bordeaux, Paris and even Australia buy up the old farms and make modern-style wine.

Also worth noting are the *vins de pays*. These give a name to print on the label to wines that once went into blends. Some are no better than they were then, but others use the identity to stress flavour and character. Many *vins de pays* are made from newly-introduced grapes. They are allowed to use the grape name (in contrast to AOC wines) and the stress on Cabernet Sauvignon would make a Californian feel at home.

Hidden amid the mass-market wines are a few classy estates, where New World-style pioneering spirit has been grafted onto French *terroir* and tradition. The leader is Mas de Daumas Gassac in the Hérault region with its stunningly good red wines, but others are catching up. They work within appellations such as Minervois and St-Chinian, and in the *vin de pays* zones which surround and overlap them. Clues to quality are stress on grape names, estate bottling and label

PROVENCE

The potential is there, but so far Languedoc is beating Provence in the race to make good, modern everyday wine. Some corners, such as Cassis and Bandol, make old-fashioned, even classic, reds; but much of Provence turns out rosé which mostly could be better. Some estates in the Côtes de Provence zone make fine reds, having added classic grapes such as Cabernet to the local specialities, but they are in a minority.

CORSICA

Beyond the southern horizon from the Côte d'Azur lies the island of Corsica, part of France but with a strong identity and, in wine terms, many links with Italy. Wines made here are rarely found on the mainland, but they can be well worth trying. Modern producers in the north make fresh, flavoursome whites and soft reds from international grape varieties using the name Vin de Pays de l'Ile de Beauté. Other estates make the traditional red wines of the island from grapes found nowhere else. Ajaccio and Patrimonio are two districts reckoned to make better wine than the overall Vin de Corse AOC.

WINE REGIONS OF ITALY

Near Panzano in Chianti.

IF FRANCE IS THE MOTHER OF WINE, Italy has a fair claim to being the father. It was the Romans, after all, who carried the vine with them into every corner of their empire which could be persuaded to grow it. And Italy today, in most years, produces even more than France.

Wine is made in every Italian region, and drunk at virtually every table. Most Italians, and most foreigners, take it at its simplest: a litre bottle with a screw cap from the grocery store, a well-known name such as Soave or Chianti in a restaurant. Many Italians are able to buy wine locally, direct from the farm, so pervasive is the crop in the landscape. Bottles and labels are recent arrivals in the Italian countryside.

Viewed as more than a mere commodity, a staple, Italian wine can be a lifetime's study. It is an enormously complex world, confusingly organized, with thousands of different wines and a vast network of producers and merchants. It is very easy to be dismissive of the whole scene, invoking clichés about chaotic Italy to justify sweeping ignorance. To turn aside from something so central to Italian life is to miss much. If the label reveals the who and where, the locals, at least, can judge the quality of the wine. The rest of us have some studying to do.

How, then, do non-Italians (and even Italian city-dwellers) get to grips with the cornucopia of flavours? The first step is to outwit the wine trade. Those who sell Italian wine, especially through restaurants, have decided that too much choice is bad for business. The wine lists repeat the same tired refrain of Soave and Frascati for whites, Valpolicella and Chianti for reds. There is nothing wrong with good examples of these wines — but these are blanket names: Chianti can come from a whole province. It may be very good indeed, but the name alone is no guarantee. As everywhere, one needs to look for the name of the maker, and perhaps also the location of the estate or vineyard, to know from a label if this is a good Chianti or a poor one.

This puts the onus on the merchant. Even the most avid *amateur* cannot cope with more than one region of Italy at a time. It may be possible to encompass Chianti, with its seven zones and hundreds of wine estates, each with several wines. But not, surely, Piedmont as well. A dedicated specialist in the wine trade can keep in touch with the myriad wines and estates. Spot these people by their insistence on individual wines in their lists: they will name the grower, the vineyard, the estate as well as the broad area of origin.

Italian red wines seem designed to go with food. There is often a hint of bitterness on the finish, which is very appetizing. Whites used to be flat and unexciting: modern techniques now tend to make them brisk and unexciting, though there is now a welcome trend to compromise between old and new styles. More white wines with character are now emerging, both local specialities and wines in the international mode. Italian oddities include sweet, strong reds for after-dinner drinking, and a profusion of sweet whites, especially from the south of the country.

ITALIAN WINE NAMES

There are more than 200 official wine zones. They overlap and inter-twine, so that a farmer may have the right to make six or ten types of wine from one estate. Not all the names are used, but many other (unofficial) names are used too. Wine from one of these 200 official zones carries the words *denominazione di origine controllata* — meaning it comes from a defined zone, and is made in a specified way from certain grapes. Where a DOC wine is labelled *classico* it comes from the central, supposedly best, part of the area. Some zones have been promoted from DOC to DOCG (G for *garantita* or guaranteed).

The law is changing, with a radical revision being introduced over a period of years. DOC and DOCG accolades will become more meaningful, and top wines will be able to state their vineyard and/or estate origin (as in the *crus* or châteaux of France).

The most basic wines are labelled *vino da tavola* (table wine) and these, under the new law, cannot make any claims about where they come from. IGT wines (*indicazione geografica tipica*) are like French *vins de pays*: local wines, from an area large or small, with the grape name on the label.

Brunello di Montalcino wines on sale in Italy: the purple seals over the neck capsules show that the wine is entitled to the DOCG (Denominazione di Origine Controllata e Garantita).

SWITZERLAND

AUSTRIA

TRENTINO -
ALTO ADIGE

**FRIULI-
VENEZIA
GIULIA**

SLOVENIA

VALLE
D'AOSTA

LOMBARDY
• Milan

VENETO

• Trieste

PIEMONTE

• Turin

Po

• Venice

CROATIA

• Asti

FRANCE

LIGURIA
• Genoa

Modena •

EMILIA-ROMAGNA
• Bologna

• Ravenna

SAN MARINO

Pisa •

Arno
• Florence

• Ancona

TOSCANA

MARCHES

UMBRIA

A D R I A T I C

Tiber

Pescara •

S E A

LAZIO

ABRUZZO

• ROME

MOLISE

Bari •

Naples •

CAMPANIA

APULIA

BASILICATA

SARDINIA

M E D I T E R R A N E A N

S E A

CALABRIA

• Cagliari

N

Palermo •

Messina •

0   200 kms

0   100 miles

SICILY

• Catania

At present, some of the most expensive Italian wines are humbly labelled as *vino da tavola*. This is because the old DOC rules disqualified wines made from non-traditional grapes. So pioneers in Tuscany who wanted to experiment with Cabernet Sauvignon and Chardonnay vines had to demote the results to the lowest grade. This did not stop them inventing impressive names, using heavy glass bottles and charging high prices. The quality, and novelty, of the wines ensured them a market. (Now some makers reckon that novelty is all that's needed, so do not take all fancy bottles at face value.)

The 'super' *vini da tavola* — as they became known — were, however, the catalyst for the change in the law. In an elegant gesture, the authorities have just added Sassicaia, the original non-DOC superstar, to the ranks of DOCs.

Most Italian wine makes no claims to quality, official or otherwise. Only about one bottle in every eight is in the DOC/DOCG sector. The IGT grade may sort out some local characters from the anonymous mass, just as *vin de pays* has done in France.

These vineyards at Castello di Volpaia in the Chianti district are high, and thus have a cool climate: Chardonnay and Sauvignon Blanc are therefore grown for white vino da tavola wines.

An understanding of some terms which may appear on labels makes Italian wine more comprehensible. *Abboccato* means medium-sweet, *Dolce* means sweet. *Bricco* (in Piedmont) means a good vineyard, one on a hill. *Riserva* wine has been aged for a certain number of months or years, as laid down in the local DOC, and is by implication better for it. *Secco* means dry, *Superiore* promises more alcohol, and longer ageing, than the basic DOC wine.

UNDERSTANDING THE REGIONS

The map shows Italy's mountainous character. Flat land is rare — and the plains of the Po, in the north, are about the only area without vineyards. From parched Sicily, where the heat is African, to the borders of Switzerland, where the vines cling to Alpine slopes, there is wine. The twenty governmental regions are used to make some sense of the profusion. But there is nothing in the law that says that a

wine must carry its regional name on the label. So listing the wines of, say, Tuscany all together is just a wine encyclopedist's convenience.

There *are* regional identities, and it is helpful to think of vinous Italy in four sections. These are the north, on the fringes of the Po Valley; what might be called Greater Tuscany in the centre; the east coast; and the south.

THE NORTH OF ITALY

The north comes first, both in geography and quality. There are few vines in the Po Valley, that great plain where rice and corn are the crops. The vines stand in a great ring where the ground rises to the Alps in the north and the Apennines in the south. The mountains moderate the otherwise hot summers and provide plenty of vine-friendly slopes.

The north-west forms one clear unit. The wine country of Piedmont, home of red Barolo and sparkling Asti, is tucked into the hilly corner between the Alps and the Apennines. Barolo and Barbaresco, near Alba, are the best-known areas, making red wines from the Nebbiolo grape, one of Italy's

The vineyards in the Valle d'Aosta in northern Italy are among the highest in Europe. The pergolas, with wooden bars resting on rough stone pillars, are traditional in the valley.

(indeed, Piedmont's) unique specialities. These wines used to be tough, hard-to-enjoy monsters which needed years of ageing — and even then sometimes failed to show much charm. Recent vintages have seen more fluid, accessible wines which win friends for their ability to partner food. This part of Italy believes in long, rich meals, and provides the wines to go with them. Nebbiolo is grown elsewhere in the north-west for wines which have some of the character, if not the overwhelming power, of Barolo. As experiments in California show, this is an under-rated red wine grape. Other Piedmont wines include a clutch of light reds with the name of the Dolcetto grape on the label, and other more thoughtful reds labelled Barbera. White wines here include the still, dry Gavi and the frothy, usually sweet Asti.

The tangle of DOC boundaries in Piedmont irresistibly brings to mind a plate of pasta. There are dozens of wines, red white and pink. Many can show (in good hands) interest,

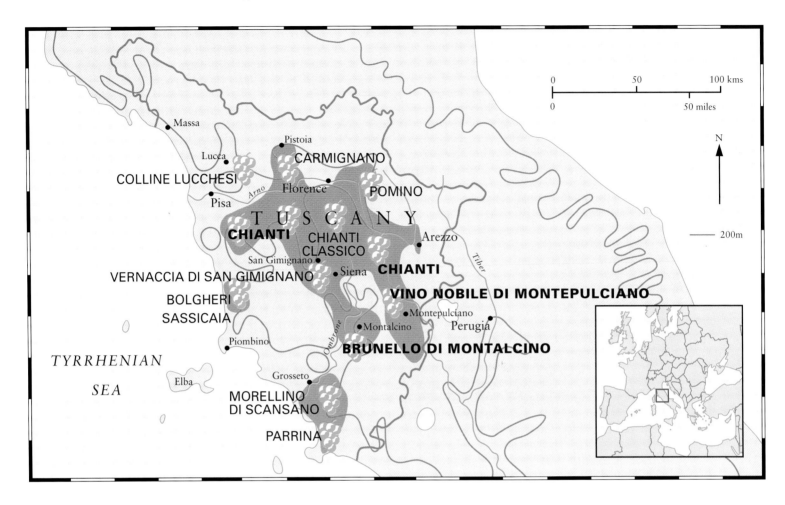

value and flavour. The prosperous citizens of Milan and Turin comb this countryside for the next fashionable grower and the newest wines: if you have a good Italophile wine merchant, you can enjoy them too.

Nearby Lombardy also makes wine, but of lesser stature. The sparkling wines from around Brescia are however perhaps Italy's best. Look for the words *metodo classico* to denote the use of the champagne method. The Oltrepò Pavese hills make lots of reliable red and white wines, but the Milanese drink most of them.

Further east, the Veneto — the hinterland of Venice — has several famous names: white Soave, and the twin reds Valpolicella and Bardolino. These wine zones lie to the east of the beautiful Lake Garda. There is a gulf here between the mass-produced wines and those of proud estates, often small. The latter can be excellent, especially Soave and Valpolicella from the *classico* zones. Valpolicella, like Chianti, comes in several styles, from easy-to-quaff café wine through age-worthy reds to the esoteric Recioto, a rich red made from semi-dried grapes that the locals sip after dinner. Bardolino is a light red,

sometimes pink, wine to drink cool and young — at times so young as to be *novello*, Italy's answer to Beaujolais Nouveau, wine only a couple of months old. The same zone, close to Lake Garda, makes Bianco di Custoza, a white wine which competes with Soave. Just around the lake, and straddling the border with Lombardy, Lugana is another white of perhaps higher average quality.

On the eastern frontier of Italy, the Friuli region makes important amounts of good white and red wines. The best zones are called Collio Goriziano and Collio Orientali. Both are right on the Slovenian border. Wines here are from local and northern European grapes: the best whites are Tocai (not from Pinot Gris, but a unique local grape) and Pinot Grigio, plus Chardonnay; leading reds are Cabernet and Merlot. Unusually, all the DOC wines here are from single varieties, with blends not allowed. Isonzo and Carso are two more DOC zones to note from this high-quality region.

The final northern region is the Trentino-Alto Adige, a

Right: new vineyards among the age-old landscape of Italy, here in Basilicata in the south.
Above: the map shows the wine zones of Tuscany.

country of deep valleys that lead on north through the Alps to Austria. Wines here have a brisk, fruity-but-dry character. This is the birthplace of the Gewürztraminer grape, which spread to Germany and, famously, Alsace. It came from the village of Tramin, and the Gewürz- part of the name is left off here. Other whites from Riesling, Pinot Grigio and increasingly Chardonnay. Reds are more idiosyncratic and less appreciated outside the valleys. Many of the people here speak German, as place-names attest, and much of the wine is exported to Austria and Germany.

CENTRAL ITALY

The great mountain range that takes up so much of Italy provides plenty of foothills and valleys to shelter vines. The western side of the country, north of Rome, centres around the big region of Tuscany, which has some outstanding wines. Florence, Pisa and Lucca, and dozens of smaller cities, have been centres of civilisations since before the Romans, and the

wines have venerable pedigrees. Chianti is a sprawling wine zone with a heartland (*classico*) and several sub-zones. All Chianti is classed as DOCG; not all deserves to be. All Chianti is red, but that is all it has in common; with some wines made for drinking in a few months and others which makers hope you will cellar for 20 years.

Chianti Classico is the core of the wine zone, with the most beautiful wooded hills, the best vineyards and the most renowned estates. Alongside DOCG Chianti Classico many of these estates make *vini da tavola*, red wines which add 'foreign' grapes such as Cabernet Sauvignon to the Tuscan staples. The beautiful cities of Florence and Siena can also call on Chianti from the Colli Fiorentini and Rufina, and from the Colli Senesi. Carmignano, from near Florence, is a fine red with an (official) dash of Cabernet. The other great Tuscan reds are Brunello, from Montalcino, and Vino Nobile from Montepulciano. Brunello is a substantial, expensive wine; its neighbour only a little less so. Both have junior reds, the *Rossi* of Montepulciano and Montalcino, at easier prices.

White wine in Tuscany has a harder time making itself known. Vernaccia di San Gimignano is the only one with a reputation: wines normally refreshing and crisp, occasionally solid and serious. Tuscany has a unique offering in Vin Santo, a sweet wine (a few are dry) made from dried grapes. The wine is left in a special small barrel for up to six years. It can be nectar, from the best growers, but can equally be an odd, sweet concoction.

Umbria, next door to Tuscany, has a similar environment and makes lesser but comparable wines. White Orvieto, when well made, is as good as any Tuscan white (which is not saying that much) The *classico* zone is the best. Around Rome, Latium (Lazio in Italian) has always concentrated on satisfying the thirst of Rome for light, easy wines. Frascati is the name everyone knows: it is usually dry, but *abboccato* or gently sweet versions can be good too.

Over the mountains on the Adriatic coast, a string of vineyards in the Marche and Abruzzo regions have a unity. Rosso Cònero and Montepulciano d'Abruzzo are good-value reds, as is Verdicchio white.

Emilia-Romagna, where the broad Po Valley meets the

Vineyards in the Chianti Classico zone of Tuscany. Here are made both Chianti and a vino da tavola from pure Sangiovese.

Down in southern Italy, Aglianico del Vulture is one of the best reds.

mountains, makes large amounts of wine which is largely drunk locally. Here the food is if anything even heartier than in Piedmont, and the wine rather takes second place. This is Lambrusco country, though the fizzy sweet red exported in such vast amounts is not as good as the wine the Emilians keep for themselves. Other wines of interest come from the Colli Piacentini zone: whites and reds with personality, and often with a gentle fizz.

SOUTHERN ITALY AND THE ISLANDS

Southern Italy is another world. The climate is hotter and drier, the wine and food traditions are from Greece and North Africa rather than the lands north and west of the Alps, the wines are very different. There are plenty of venerable names, but in most cases the DOCs preserved the names and little else. Most wines have in the past been poor, aimed only at blending or even distilling into industrial alcohol, but the patches of quality are being exploited by go-ahead producers who show that good wines can be made. Like southern France (but a generation behind) this is pioneer country.

The southeast spur of Italy, Apulia (Puglia) has a growing name for good, modern red and white wines. Here, too, can be found the traditional strong, sweet wines which shadow the Ancient Greek ruins around the Mediterranean. Basilicata, Italy's most backward region, makes a good smooth red in Aglianico del Vulture.

Sicily and Sardinia share the South's problems and advantages. Sicily has the fine fortified marsala to offer. At its best, it can hold its own with madeira and port, and should not be relegated to the *zabaglione*. Sicilian table wines can be good value as investment in hyper-modern wineries by both cooperatives and private estates is bearing fruit. The tiny islands of Lipari and Pantelleria yield rich dessert wines of high quality. Sardinia is even more a world alone. The wines can be good val;ue but are are eccentric in both name and character: Monica and Cannonau are lively, sometimes slightly sweet reds; Vernaccia di Oristano is a strong, pungent dry white; Nuragus is a lighter white; various sweet Malvasias offer more flavour and authenticity.

WINE REGIONS OF GERMANY

Burg Stahleck looms above the Rhine vineyards.

COMPARED TO ITS NEIGHBOUR France, the vine is far less at home in Germany, with its cooler climate and harsher winters. Vines are grown only in a few well-sheltered valleys and are absent entirely from the north and east of the country. As a consequence, the German view of wine differs from that of France. It is far less an everyday staple, more a modest luxury. Most German wine is white, much of it designed not for meal-times but for drinking on its own. The Germans love French wine, and buy large amounts of it as they adopt more widely the 'Latin' habit of drinking wine with food. This has led to efforts to re-shape German wines to allow them to partner food more readily, and to attempts at making more red wines. The result is a wider range of German wines, and rediscovery by some other countries of their quality.

Every wine country has its wine stereotype. France nurtures the idea that each vineyard has its own unique personality, as strong as that of a Frenchman. Germany dreams of a sunny corner of a vine-clad terrace, a tall green bottle and glasses of golden wine, glinting in the sunlight. The river winds below, the tiered vineyards rise above, the wine-growers sit in their horn-buttoned jackets while the scent of something savoury drifts from the inn door. Meanwhile, cask after cask of wine ages gracefully in the rock-cut cellar beneath their feet.

In truth, the average bottle of German wine is rushed

through a winery as atmospheric as a lemonade factory, and sometimes owned by the same company. The bottling lines roar and clank while the supermarket delivery truck grumbles at the end of the conveyor belt.

German wine has fallen into the gap between these two extremes: the hand-made and the mass-produced. Many a consumer in the countries to which Germany exports its wines has shaken off the Liebfraumilch habit — this being today a blended factory wine known only to export markets and never drunk by Germans. They have moved on from sugar-and-water Mosels, for example, to fruity Australian Chardonnays. All the time, the great Rhine and Mosel vineyards and estates have been doggedly turning out superb handmade wines. Most wine drinkers failed to find them, bemused by the number of mass-market bottles between them and the good stuff.

This sad tale means that good German wines are a bargain. A new generation of growers is fighting hard to regain the quality image their grandfathers and fathers squandered in the pursuit of market share. The amount of wine made is coming down: grapes are replaced by the potatoes and sugar beet the fields are most fitted for, while the best vineyards are nowadays being cropped less heavily.

The result: wine with more flavour, which can age for longer. The point of German wine is Riesling, the great white grape that made the old-time Rhine and Mosel classics. The point of Riesling is bottle age. These wines can be deliciously fresh when young — especially on that sunny terrace — but with some years in bottle they acquire a whole new personality, losing sweetness and acquiring nutty notes to go with the fruit.

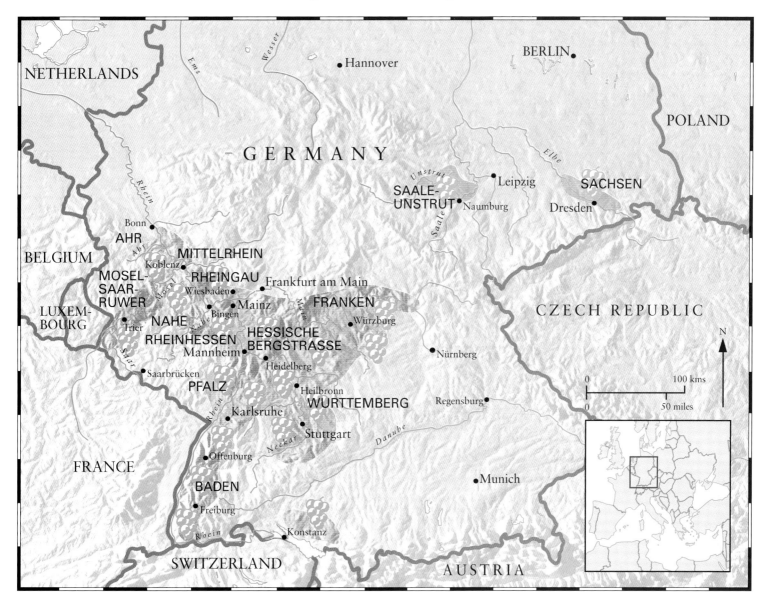

Many wine drinkers value German wines for their gentleness and medium-sweet reliability. Others avoid them for these very qualities, which they see as blandness and lack of personality. Both groups would probably enjoy 'real' German wines — from quality-conscious estates — if they only discovered them.

FINDING QUALITY

What, then, are the pointers to good wine? It is usual to split Germany up by region: there are 13 official wine zones, such as Rheingau and Pfalz, and virtually every wine label will carry the name of one of them. Within these zones are hundreds of areas and thousands of vineyards. On top of this geography the rules place a pyramid of quality grades based upon the sweetness level. This approach is a useful start but it

fails to reveal — indeed can actively conceal — which are the best wines. The grower's name and the grape variety are the keys, allied to the vintage.

To take vintages first, the year on the label matters because German vineyards are well to the north of the rest of the European wine belt. A glance at the map on page 81 shows that even the southernmost Rhine zone, Baden, is on a level with Alsace and Champagne, two of France's most northern vineyards. A cool, cloudy year means unripe grapes and wines lacking in natural fruit sugar. German law (like French) allows man to make up for nature's shortcomings by adding sugar. Wine from a warm, sunny year will have more natural sweetness (see page 31 for the various grades), more flavour and more chance of ageing well in bottle.

The grape variety matters, for there are many vines grown in Germany which put quantity before quality. The classic white-wine grape here is Riesling, and the best of the Mosel wines, and those of the Rheingau district, will be made from it. Elsewhere, other vines come into prominence, though every German zone makes some Riesling wines. In the other Rhein zones, such as Pfalz and Rheinhessen, the Ruländer grape (the Pinot Gris of Alsace), the Weissburgunder (Pinot Blanc) and the Silvaner make good white wines. Red wines are a recent passion among German winemakers, but few expert tasters outside Germany rate their efforts highly.

Good Riesling is made only from the best vineyards: those with the most sun, which means south-facing, and the most appropriate soil, which in the Mosel is slate and elsewhere is well-drained gravel, sand and other soils. Steep slopes are rated highly: the drainage will be good, the angle to the sun advantageous and cold air will also drain away, avoiding damaging spring frosts.

Finally, the name of the grower matters more and more in Germany. The great estates of the Rhein and Mosel have been joined in the ranks of quality by smaller concerns, often with go-ahead young proprietors. Many (but not all) of the top wine estates belong to the VDP, a club which uses a black eagle emblem on labels. In general, a label which stresses the name of the estate or grower, and does not hide behind a district name, should be preferred. Estates which bottle their wine often say so on the label: the German term is

Grape pickers in the steep Rhine vineyards need a good head for heights.

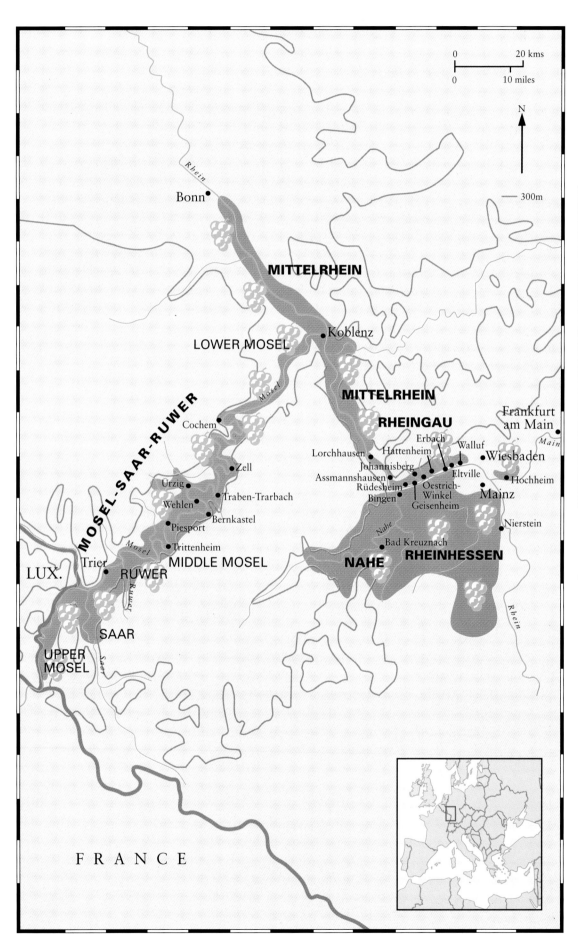

0   20 kms

0   10 miles

N

— 300m

Rhein

Bonn

MITTELRHEIN

LOWER MOSEL

Koblenz

Mosel

MITTELRHEIN

MOSEL-SAAR-RUWER

RHEINGAU

Frankfurt
am Main

Cochem

Erbach

Main

Lorchhausen

Hattenheim

Walluf

Wiesbaden

Zell

Johannisberg

Eltville

Ürzig

Assmannshausen

Hochheim

Traben-Trarbach

Rüdesheim

Oestrich-
Winkel

Mainz

Wehlen

Bingen

Geisenheim

Mosel

Piesport

Bernkastel

Nahe

Nierstein

Trittenheim

Bad Kreuznach

Trier

Ruwer

MIDDLE MOSEL

NAHE

RHEINHESSEN

LUX.

RUWER

Rhein

SAAR

Saar

UPPER
MOSEL

FRANCE

Left: the map shows the heartland of
German wine, in the Rhine and Mosel
valleys.
Above: the 14th-century Altes Haus in
the Rhine town of Bacharach.

Erzeugerabfüllung. Some 'producers' are giant cooperatives, which make adequate but rarely superlative wines.

THE REGIONS

The map on page 83 clearly shows that rivers form the skeleton of the German wine regions. A valley's often steep sides lend themselves to vineyards, often with terracing. As the Mosel, for instance, meanders through the forested hills of the Eifel, its twists and turns offer many sheltered south-facing slopes. The slopes tip the vines towards the sun, yielding the ripest grapes. Recently, less well-placed slopes, and even some flat land, have been planted with vines, but the quality is just not to be had and some are now being returned to other crops. The best-regarded vineyards of the valley are in the middle section, known as the *bereich* or district of Bernkastel but more accurately called the Mittel Mosel. Here are villages such as Whelen, Piesport, Urzig and Bernkastel itself. Their wines are known by the German convention of adding '-er' to the end of the name. The vineyard name always comes after the village name.

This raises the point that 'Piesporter', under German law, does not have to come from that village. It can be from any of the wide group of vineyards (a *grosslage*) called Piesporter Michelsberg. German wine law actually forbids labels from giving a vital clarification: whether the wine comes from a single vineyard or a group.

The only way to get round this obfuscation is to go straight for estate-bottled wines from individual growers. A few merchants have revived the idea of selling wine according to the village, not the vineyard, which was the norm a century ago. But the labyrinth of the label law makes it hard to find such honestly-named wines amid the confusion.

The Mosel has a large number of great wine estates, most of which belong to the 'Grosser Ring', a sort of guild or club. Look for the eagle badge of the VDP, which includes all the Ring members. Many other smaller concerns also bottle their own, excellent, wines.

Further upstream, the side-valleys of the Saar and Ruwer offer even more delicate Riesling wines, particularly enjoyable in warm vintages (in cold ones the wine becomes fizzy *Sekt*). Here, too, the best wines come from the estates.

All the other main wine regions are strung along the Rhine, with two exceptions: the valley of the Nahe, which joins the Rhine at Bingen, and that of the Neckar, which drains the Franken region. Nahe wine is often very good value, lacking the famous names of the Mosel and Rhine. There is some Riesling, and a wide variety of other (mostly white) grapes including Weissburgunder and Silvaner. The best wines come from the steep-sided central section of the valley around Niederhausen and Schlossböckelheim, and the top estates include the state domaine, whose Prussian eagle on the label recalls its foundation a century ago.

Franken wine is rarely found outside Germany, indeed outside its home state. The vineyards struggle in a harsher climate than the Rhine valley, and in the coldest years the amount of wine made drops steeply. Franken wine is often made dry ('trocken' is the word on the label); Silvaner is the traditional grape for white wine but a variety of others are also grown. Most of the wine is white. A custom in Franken is to use a special bottle shape: a dumpy flask called a *bocksbeutel*.

Back on the Rhine, the best vineyards are generally held to be those in the Rheingau, a broad south-facing slope west of Frankfurt. Here the Rhine runs east-west before diving into the great gorge which takes it on north to Koblenz. The Rheingau has a warm climate, ideal for ripening Riesling, and makes some of the most flavoursome and longest-lived of German white wines.

The best Rheingau villages include Rüdesheim, Johannisberg, Erbach and Eltville. Hochheim, beside the River Main, also has a fine reputation. It gave its name to 'hock', an English word for any Rhine wine.

The Rheingau has long treasured ripeness in its grapes: a warm autumn concentrates the sugar and flavour in the fruit, allowing a naturally sweet wine to be made. These wines, labelled *Spätlese* (late-picked), *Auslese* (selected) and so on, are wonderful drinks when mature. But they are too sweet for meal-times, and modern Rheingau growers want to see their wines on the top restaurant tables as well as in the cellars of a few connoisseurs. So they now stress drier wines, made to strict standards under the Charta umbrella. Charta is a club of estates: look for their name on labels as a guarantee of Riesling wines made to partner food.

The other Rhine regions are Rheinhessen, on the opposite bank to the Rheingau, with mostly everyday white wines, and the Pfalz (it used to be Rheinpfalz) where increasing amounts of good, solid white wines are made as well as some fast-improving reds. Germany's best red wines come from here and Baden. The best Rheinhessen wines are from Nierstein. Not Niersteiner Gutes Domtal, which covers a wide area, but the vineyards of the town itself Oppenheim has a similar name for good, earthy white wines. The best Pfalz villages are the string of half-timbered gems in the Mittelhaardt district, Names such as Forst, Deidesheim, Wachenheim and Ruppertsberg bring to mind solid, tasty Riesling and Silvaner white wines, increasingly made dry.

Baden is the warmest corner of Germany, and its wines reflect the climate in their depth of flavour. There are many fine vineyards around the Kaiserstuhl hills, and in villages such as Durbach and Ortenberg. The best whites are the Rieslings — here fuller, drier and more akin to Alsace in style than is normal in Germany, and the Ruländer or Pinot Gris

— 'stiff' is the word used to describe their savoury, lingering but dry flavour. The red wines come from Spätburgunder (Pinot Noir), increasingly aged in oak. They can be very good. Weissherbst, a sweet rosé, is a local favourite which tastes good on a sunny cafe terrace.

The former East Germany has added two wine regions to the national total. They are Sachsen (Saxony) and Saale-Unstrut. Neither send much wine to the outside world, but their dry, savoury whites are worth trying on the spot. Another region where local thirsts consume all the wine is Württemberg, where light, sweet reds and (more interesting) Riesling whites are made.

Vineyards of the Upper Mosel valley at Palzem.

CENTRAL & SOUTH-EAST EUROPE

In the Wachau district of Austria.

THE NORTHERN FRONTIERS of the grape vine across Europe match closely those of the Roman Empire. Legionnaires only thrived, it seems, where the vine did too. Along this invisible frontier are a string of wine lands which do not aspire to the classic heights of France and Italy, but which all have something to contribute to the wine list. Switzerland forms an alpine, or rather sub-alpine, bastion of quality wine appreciation and (to a lesser extent) production. Austria, plus its neighbours to north, east and south-east, has a strong wine culture of its own. The great River Danube flows east and south, linking wine zones in a dozen countries between Germany and the Black Sea.

SWITZERLAND AND AUSTRIA

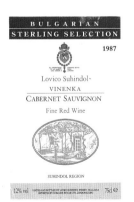

Switzerland, small though it is, is a land of intense local loyalties, with four languages and thriving democracy at Canton (county) level. This attitude applies to wine: most of the wine is drunk where it is made. Visitors to east, or German-speaking, Switzerland find wines unknown in Geneva or Lausanne at the other end of the country. Thereabouts, in the French-speaking west, they make the few wines non-Swiss may hear of: the full-bodied whites and juicy reds of the Valais, the Alpine valley of the upper Rhône, and the Vaud, the district beside Lake Geneva. Down in the south, where

Wine regions of Switzerland and Austria.

Italian is the language, the Ticino district makes interesting reds from Merlot grapes. The eastern wines stress Germanic white grapes and some reds from Pinot Noir (which they call Blauburgunder).

Austria makes more wine — enough for both local thirsts and exports — and with a wider choice of sites and climates it also makes more of a range than Switzerland. The vines are in the eastern third of the country, around Vienna and close to the frontiers of countries which (until 1918) were part of Austria. There is no real border between the vineyards of the Burgenland in east Austria and those of Sopron in western Hungary. No more real is the divide between Styria and Slovenia, or between the Weinviertel of Lower Austria and the Czech Republic. The interested wine lover can follow the wine styles right down the Danube.

What are these styles? In Austria, it is hard to be categorical. Most wine is white, but red wines command the attention of some of the best producers and as a result are growing better all the time. Much Austrian white wine is dry and appetizing, but some of the best are honey-sweet. If Austria has a speciality, it is the kind of white wine which Alsace also perfects: powerful and dry enough to go with food, and at the same time fruity and flowery enough to drink alone.

These are Germanic wines for those who do not like German wines. The best are from Riesling, and the native Austrian grapes such as Grüner Veltliner. The Wachau, a scenic and hilly tract along the Danube, makes the best of these. Although 'classic' grapes such as Chardonnay have made inroads, these express the Austrian wine character less clearly. Other white wines of interest are those from Weissburgunder (Pinot Blanc), Rülander (Pinot Gris) and Muscat Ottonel. Sweet wines from late-picked, over-ripe grapes, labelled *Beerenauslese* and *Trockenbeerenauslese* as in Germany, are made in large amounts in the Burgenland region, and can be excellent. Austrian red wines command high prices, with fashionable makers, new-oak barrels and designer labels in a positive New World-style fuss, but non-Austrians find it hard to equate value and price.

In the cellars of Tokay: note the mould-covered walls – this particular fungus thrives on the wine fumes.

HUNGARY AND ITS NEIGHBOURS

Hungary is, in history, geography and wine, the other half of Austria. They were twin countries for centuries, under the same crown. The estates were owned by the same great families, and the wine traded by the same merchants. Hungary, however, has a strong wine tradition of its own as well as grapes and styles in common with Austria.

The wine at the head of any Hungarian list is Tokay, made far away on the eastern frontier, where the Ukraine, Slovakia and Hungary meet. Here a tradition of sweet white wine using late-picked grapes has been evolving for 300 years. The misty autumns of this riverside vineyard (compare with Sauternes, page 46) allow the same 'noble rot', *botrytis cineria*, to develop. The raisiny, shrivelled, or *aszú*, grapes are kept

apart from the merely over-ripe ones. The *aszú* grapes are then added, in various proportions, to the wine made from the ordinary ripe fruit.

The more *aszú* grapes, the higher the number of *puttonyos* (the traditional name for the basket in which the grapes were collected; now an indicator of the level of sweetness). This mixture begins to ferment for a second time, making the wine more powerful, richer and sweeter.

Most Tokay is made at three to six *puttonyos*. The sweetest of Tokays is Aszú Essencia, which is about as sweet and powerful in flavour as a wine can get. The fabled Essencia, which has (in legend at least) revived several dying kings, is still made — but never sold. It comes from undiluted *aszú* grapes, and to taste it is more honey than wine.

Some dry Tokay, labelled Szamorodni, is made. It can be very good: dense, rich yet dry in the Hungarian fashion. These dry wines appear in normal-size bottles: the *aszú* Tokays use 50cl bottles.

Elsewhere in Hungary the enquiring visitor will find many fascinating wines, mostly white and ranging from medium dry to medium sweet. The native grape varieties are the most interesting — if hardest to pronounce. Large areas have been planted with Chardonnay, Sauvignon Blanc and other 'classic' grapes to meet the demand from western buyers. These wines are sometimes excellent, but hardly Hungarian. Red wines in Hungary are improving, leaving behind the somewhat stale legend of Bull's Blood, which (like so many legends) is not what it was.

The vine is at home in most of Hungary, a land lacking mountains. The area around Lake Balaton has a good name for both traditional and modern-style wines. The huge Balatonboglar experimental farm is here, on the south shore, turning out large amounts of very reasonable Chardonnay.

North of Hungary is Slovakia, a country which shares many of the grapes and wine styles of its neighbour. The Tokay vineyards actually cross the frontier, but Slovakian Tokay is a rare wine indeed. The Little Carpathians region in the west of the country (Malokapartska on the map) makes good white wines. Pezinok and Modra, in particular, have good wineries. Other useful wines come from around Nitra.

Further north-west, the Czech Republic makes enjoyable white wines in Moravia and Bohemia (north of Prague). The wines here are more Austrian in character, with Grüner

Veltliner among the grapes grown. Most Czech wine is drunk in Prague's cafés, where the beer too is excellent.

To the south, the new country of Slovenia has a good name for white wine. Many remember the Ljutomer wines from the days when this land was part of Yugoslavia. Now these, though still good, are being overshadowed by wines from the Primorski region, in the west, where the vineyards run on across the frontier from the Italian Collio zone. Red wines are good here, with Merlot and Cabernet, plus whites from Pinot Gris. Slovenia should be a name to watch in the future.

BULGARIA AND ROMANIA

The Danube divides these two large, very different and virtually unknown lands. Both were locked deep into Communist eastern Europe for 40 years, but they followed different paths in wine as in much else. Romania, which being further from Constantinople achieved its freedom from the Turks earlier, had the stronger wine tradition. In the early years of the 20th century Romanian wine had a name for quality as far west as Paris. Bulgaria, which only began its wine industry after 1918, had no real traditions. However Bulgaria's freedom

from the baggage of the past made it open to new grape varieties and techniques. While Romania spent the Communist years making poor wine and drinking it at home, Bulgaria set out to conquer Western markets with good-value wines. Vast vineyards of Cabernet Sauvignon, Merlot, Chardonnay and other 'classic' grapes were planted. Production facilities, while workmanlike, never caught up with the best of the New World, but the wine was very good value and achieved ready acceptance.

Today the picture is more complex. Bulgaria still makes and sells lots of good everyday wine. But the once enormous Russian market has vanished, and many vineyards have had to be dug up as there was no outlet for their wine. Bulgarian wineries now have aspirations to quality, and an elaborate system of quality grades is in place. *Controliran* wines are the rough equivalent of AOC or DOC wine in France and Italy. Special Reserve and Reserve wines are selected bottlings, with more ageing than other wines. The calibre of the maker, rather than the quality grade on the label, is the

information worth knowing about modern Bulgarian wines.

While the Bulgarian wineries are grouped into regions (see map on page 89), it is hard to generalize about local characteristics. Much depends upon the wineries, or rather the people running them. The best white wines seem to come from the eastern region, along the Black Sea coast, in particular from Preslav and Khan Krum. Good reds come from Suhindol and Russe in the northern region, along the Danube.

Romania has a complex array of native grapes, with names even harder to grasp than the Hungarians. Some Western 'classics' have done well, notably Pinot Noir in the Dealul Mare region. The hills of Transylvania offer cool, well-placed sites for a wide range of whites and reds, including Pinot Gris and Sauvignon Blanc. Cotnari, which a century ago was a sweet white wine to rival Tokay, is still made, but lacks distinction. The potential for quality is there, but Romania has a long road to travel.

THE BLACK SEA

One of the oddest developments since 1990 has been the emergence of Moldova as a source of fine red wines. The western world learned that the Soviet government had encouraged the planting of Cabernet Sauvignon and other French grapes in Moldova, then a part of the USSR and now somewhat precariously independent. Following independence, venerable and delicious bottles began to emerge from the former state cellars. It is clear from these 20-year-old wines that high potential is there, but many obstacles (a shortage of bottles and corks, for a start) stand between Moldova and a consistent, modern wine industry. Elsewhere in the former Soviet Union, both the Ukraine and Russia have large vineyards. The Crimea (at the time of writing, part of Ukraine) has a tradition of fine sweet wines: the Tsars kept a wonderfully stocked cellar at Massandra, complete with copies of every sweet Western wine from port to Sauternes.

Georgia and Armenia make wine, mostly following local traditions which, though fascinating to historians, do not yield results in tune with international tastes. Further into Central Asia, vineyards grow on the shores of the Caspian and beside cities founded by Alexander the Great. Their produce is the stuff of travellers' tales.

The beautiful gold of Five Puttonyos Tokay.

SPAIN & PORTUGAL

The palace of Mateus, Portugal.

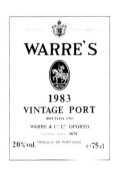

THE VINE, SO MUCH AT HOME in Spain and Portugal, is losing ground to the brewery and the fizzy-drink factory — and this is good news. As in Italy and France, habits are changing as more people adapt to a city-based lifestyle. Beer and soft drinks are gaining at the expense of the familiar litre of red plonk as everyday thirst-quenchers, leaving wine for wine lovers. The quality of wine has to rise — and is rising — if the thirsty farm workers are to be replaced as customers.

A generation ago Spain had only one quality wine zone, Rioja. Plenty of superb fortified sherry was made, but among table wines only red Rioja was really of international calibre. There were good wines made elsewhere, but they were rarely exported. Other Spanish wines were either rustic survivals or mass-produced blends at the lower end of the quality scale. Portugal was much the same, with lots of local characters, and oceans of everyday wine; but only (fortified) port to offer the international connoisseur.

Fortified wines are still Iberia's greatest contribution to the world wine list, and they are covered separately on pages 96-98. But we can now also look to Spain and Portugal for good and unusual white and red wines, both at the table wine and the fine wine levels.

The map shows that few places in either country are without vineyards. Several mountain ranges cross the peninsula, running east-west, dividing the great land mass into distinct zones from north to south. The west, exposed to the Atlantic, is cooler and wet; the south and east take their weather from the Mediterranean and are hot and dry. The wines show this pattern: the best whites are from the cool, damp north, while fortified wines stem from the south, around Malaga and Jerez. The port country, despite being in the west of the peninsula, is cut off from the Atlantic by a mountain range which blocks much of the rain. Portugal's Douro Valley can be very hot and dry indeed in summer.

Many of the quality vineyards of Spain are set on high ground: the rolling plateaux which divide the mountains. Rioja and Ribera del Duero are examples: here the vineyards are high and cool, with low night-time temperatures even in the height of summer. These cool nights help concentrate flavour in the ripening grapes. Other quality zones are in the hills of the north-east, where Barcelona demands and gets good wine. The foothills of the Pyrenees, from Navarra eastward, are emerging as a source of modern wines. The best zones heave earned official recognition as *denominación de*

origen (DO). One DO, Rioja, has been promoted to DOC (the C stands for *calificada*). Ordinary table wines are categorized as *vino de mesa*, sometimes with a local name added but usually without any claim to origin. *Vino de la tierra* is the term for wines from a specific area: rather like French *vin de pays* country.

RIOJA AND THE NORTH

The Ebro, one of the great rivers of Spain, drains into the Mediterranean but rises a few miles from the Atlantic. It is still a junior river, tumbling through a gorge, where its upland valley widens to form the Rioja vineyards. Here the French frontier, as well as the ocean, are close at hand. France has contributed customers (especially in the days when Bordeaux's vineyards were blighted by the phylloxera louse), ideas and grapes. The relative sophistication of Rioja, both in making and selling wine, comes in part from France.

The red wines are sold both as un-aged (*sin crianza*) and aged (*crianza*). The best wines spend some time (it can be years) in oak barrels before bottling. These are the *reservas* and *gran reservas*. These top wines, from good vintages, can age further in bottle and are a wonderful drink. Many wine lovers appreciate the light, smooth but oaky austerity of *reserva* Rioja. The young wines are enjoyable in a different way: fresh, still light, but with fruit rather than oak. Few Riojas approach that old 'Spanish plonk' taste of alcoholic ink.

White Rioja is less easy for non-natives to admire. Good, fresh modern ones are made, but they have to work hard to out-class other white wines. The traditional white Rioja style is yellow rather than white, reeking of oak and tasting of butter, walnuts and yet more oak. An acquired taste.

Other areas in the north of Spain make good red wines. Navarra is Rioja's neighbour, and competitor at all but the *reserva* and *gran reserva* levels. There is good rosé (*rosada*) here too. White wines may well outshine those of Rioja if experiments with new grape varieties produce the expected results. Somontano, to the east, is another foothills zone with a new name for fresh whites and reds in the international, rather than Spanish traditional, style. Cariñena, further south, is a useful source of good-value wines.

To the south-west of the Ebro valley, over yet another mountain range, the Duero river flows west to the Atlantic (once across the border, the Portuguese know it as the Douro — the home of port). At the Spanish end, the high plains east of Valladolid, ancient university city and royal capital, make fine red wines. They are from Tempranillo, the grape of Rioja, which here is called Tinto Fino. The quality tradition is there, but had almost died out (with one resounding exception: Vega Sicilia with its fabulous, and fabulously expensive, wine) until the 1970s saw a revival. Now the name Ribera del Duero is a signal for good-value red wines, with some real stars among the *reservas*. Nearby Rueda makes competent white wines in the modern, fruity style.

Unusual and flavoursome white wines come from the far north-west of Spain, the part which is as green as Ireland and almost as wet. Look for, and try, Albariño: a dense, chewy kind of white. Txakoli (Chacolí) is a drier cousin from the Basque country.

Over on the east coast, Catalonia has fine traditions for dark, dessert-style wines (the Priorato of Tarragona) and sparkling ones (the Cava wines of St-Sadurni). The Cava wines are gaining extra flavour and character as makers add a dash of Chardonnay to the traditional, and rather neutral, grapes. Production is by the classic method, and the top Cavas can be very impressive. Good table wines are also made, but few other concerns have joined the Torres family in the race to international acceptance. Torres's red and white wines offer a remarkable range: many styles, all excellent.

THE CENTRE AND SOUTH

This is where the Mediterranean really takes over the climate management. Summers are hot and dry — too hot for delicate white wines. Modern techniques have made the plains of La Mancha suitable for making reliable whites and rather more fruity reds than were traditional. This can be an excellent source of everyday wine: the names used for reds are Valdepeñas and Jumilla. The whites are good value if made by one of the well-equipped cooperatives that have responded to the call for fresh, fruity, clean wines. Some have failed to heed the call — but these wines will only be found in Spain itself.

Down in the south, Malaga makes powerful and mostly sweet wines that at their best can compare with sherry. Valencia, up the coast, offers some good Muscat sweet whites.

The holiday islands, the Balearics and Canaries, have vineyards which cater well to summertime thirsts, but which produce few wines which are worth exporting.

PORTUGAL

PORTUGAL IS A NEW ENTRANT on the world wine stage. It has been making, and drinking, its own wines for centuries, of course. Many of the grapes grown in Portugal were unique, and thus the wines had strong local characters. But only fortified port and madeira made it onto the world's wine list. Now they are being joined by some good, fresh red and white table wines.

The wine laws here work according to the normal European pattern, with the 13 best zones granted a *denominação de origem controlada* (DOC) with 31 lesser zones granted *indicação de provenencia regulamentada* (IPR) status. *Garrafeira* wines are superior, matured, versions of DOC wines.

Portugal has a wide range of climates and soils, from the cool, wet northwest to the baking plains of the south. There are conditions for just about every kind of wine, and indeed there are few styles known to the world of wine which Portugal does not offer.

The north of the country took the lead in selling wine to the outside world, perhaps spurred on by the traditions of port (see page 96). Pink wine, in the odd-shaped bottle adopted by the firm of Mateus, won many a friend in the

Oporto, Portugal's second city, is the centre of the port trade: these traditional river boats show port makers' names.

1950s and 1960s, then went out of fashion. Vinho Verde, the fresh light white from the same northern area, also had its moment of fame. It may not be so fashionable now, but there are some very interesting and tasty wines made. The native northern Portuguese grapes such as Alvarinho confer a crisp, dessert-apple flavour. Vinho verde ('Verde', or green, refers to its youth, not its colour: there are red ones as well as whites) must be drunk young and fresh, and it is still true that the best wines stay where they are made.

Recently, an influx of money and ideas has started to coax good red wines out of the beautiful northern Portuguese vineyards. The port estates of the Douro, places of legendary hospitality, realised long ago that their guests cannot drink heavy, alcoholic port all the time, so they demanded and got good reds. A few of these wines escaped to London or New York, but most were appreciated on the spot. Now some are being made for the export markets: look for the Douro name on the label. They are made from the traditional port grapes, and as might be expected are rich, dark and fruity. They age well — but not quite as long as vintage port.

The centre of Portugal is noted for its red wines. Dão, which with the Douro is the country's other great red wine district, is making better wine since some of the makers were persuaded not to age their reds for so long. Modern wineries and storage facilities are helping to enhance the quality of the ordinary wines, mostly made by cooperatives and marketed by merchant firms, while a rash of new estates is bringing the château concept to the region. Some growers are adding a proportion of non-Portuguese grapes, such as Cabernet Sauvignon, for added flavour.

The white wines of Dão also have a long way to come, but at their best are savoury and intense. Bairrada is another zone to the west of Dão, offering good solid red wines, typically fruitier than Dão, which can age well in bottle. Whites are made here, too, from among others the aromatic Maria Gomes grape. Such whites are solid, fruity and full of flavour: ideal with Portuguese food.

In the south of Portugal it's pot luck: good, novel wines are being made, sometimes by non-Portuguese wine makers (a clutch of Australians, for instance); but the quality has yet to settle down. Try anything odd with a Portuguese label, for experiment's sake — but don't expect the wine to be the same two years running. The Alentejo, a vast plain, is being touted

Picking grapes for Vinho Verde near Amarante in the Minho region.

as a region to watch. Great investment in modern winemaking facilities has, however, yet to be matched by improved vineyard techniques. A decade ago there was no good wine from here; now there is quite a lot, but consistency is still lacking. Despite some successes with whites from imported 'classic' grape varieties, the best Alentejo wines are red. These are solid, characterful wines, again perfect with the pungent taste of Portuguese cuisine.

Over near Lisbon, Sétubal is a traditional region for sweet white wines, now joined by dry Muscats and some modern red wines. This is also the home of Lancers, the 'other' Portuguese rosé which competes around the world with Mateus.

The Algarve has a few vineyards between the hotels and the golf courses, but despite a near-ideal climate few notable wines have emerged from the four local DOC regions. A committed winemaker might change that one day.

FORTIFIED WINES

SPAIN AND PORTUGAL MAY NOT have invented fortified wine — that credit goes to the Romans who used concentrated wine, and later the Arabs, who invented distillation — but they have dominated the making of them for the last 500 years. Sherry, from the town of Jerez in southern Spain, was the 'sherris sack' of Shakespeare, and port was invented by the British and Dutch merchants trading in Portugal three centuries ago. These hot southern lands have long made their living selling warming winter wines to the chilly North.

There is less call today for these wines, as they are strong in alcohol and partner food less readily than do lighter, softer table wines. To the wine lover, this decline in fashion is the signal for a bargain. Indeed, sherry in particular is an enormously undervalued wine.

To fortify a wine, the winemaker quite simply adds brandy or a similar spirit. This was first done to stabilise wine intended for shipping. Winemakers did not understand the fermentation process (it was only mastered in the second half of the 20th century) and many wines started to re-ferment when shaken up by transport. The resulting vinegar was not what the customers had ordered. Shippers began to dose the wine with brandy to settle it down. The resulting wine was powerful, durable and good to drink — so fortification became an accepted part of the recipe.

PORT

In port's case, fortification is carried out before the new wine has finished fermenting. The makers simply add 100 litres of brandy to each 450 litres of wine. The spirit halts the fermentation, which would otherwise have gone on until all the grape sugar was consumed, and the result is a rich, dark, spirity wine with a lot of its natural sweetness intact.

Port needs time to allow the spirit, wine and sweetness to become reconciled, and port makers allow most of their wine to age in giant casks or tanks for at least three years. It is then either bottled, as ruby port, or allowed to age for longer, when it becomes tawny port with an age claim: 10-year-old, 20-year-old and so on.

A very small amount of port is bottled when still young, and allowed to age in bottle not wood. This is vintage port, the pinnacle of quality and the only port (but see below) which claims a specific year on the label. Vintage takes at least a decade to become drinkable, and should be decanted (see page 26) as it develops a deposit in the bottle. Only the best years yield true vintage port: in most years all the wine is blended, rather as in Champagne.

After vintage, tawny and ruby (the three main branches of the port tree), port confuses its customers with a further range of styles and names. Broadly, if a bottle holds vintage port it will say so, often with the year of bottling, two years after the vintage year, on the label. Vintage-character port does not claim a single year: it is a blend of several, but in the vintage style. 'Late-bottled vintage' is responsible for some confusion. It does have a year on the label, but it is not true vintage, as it has not matured in the bottle. It is a good ruby from a single year. Its advantage, apart from price, is that it lacks the heavy deposit of vintage and can be more easily enjoyed by the glass — a boon to the restaurant trade. The occasional single-vintage tawny is bottled: these are often found in Portugal and are called *colheita* ports.

Enjoy port, vintage or vintage-character, or tawny, after dinner, as tradition demands — but also try a 10-year-old tawny slightly chilled as an apéritif. White port is one of Portugal's well-kept secrets: enjoy a dry one (some are sweet) as the port shippers do: as a lovely long drink with lemon, ice and soda or tonic.

The port country, mapped on the opposite page, is a wild and beautiful place. The grapes are grown on vertiginous terraced vineyards which clothe the sides of great hills. Below is the deep gorge of the Douro river, today a series of lakes. Tourists are slowly discovering this magic land, aided by cruise boats on the river and a splendidly old-fashioned train.

The wine, too, must make this journey, from the remote mountain vineyards down the great river (originally by sailboat), to the shippers' 'lodges' at Vila Nova de Gaia, Oporto. Here, at the river's mouth, it matures into port and is shipped around the world. The great port firms are known as 'shippers', but generally own vineyards (and buy in wine and grapes from trusted suppliers), make and market the port.

The wine estates are called *quintas* — the map shows

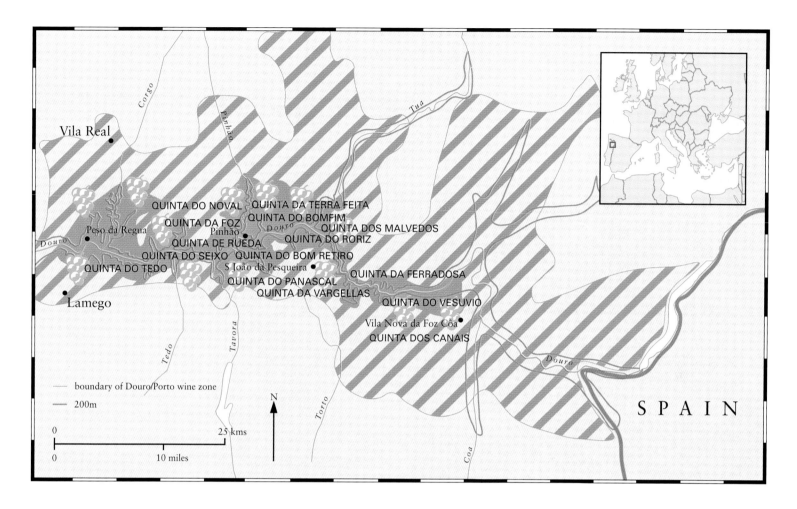

QUINTA DO NOVAL QUINTA DA TERRA FEITA
QUINTA DA FOZ QUINTA DO BOMFIM
Peso da Regua QUINTA DOS MALVEDOS
Pinhão QUINTA DO RORIZ
QUINTA DE RUEDA
QUINTA DO SEIXO QUINTA DO BOM RETIRO
QUINTA DO TEDO S João da Pesqueira QUINTA DA FERRADOSA
QUINTA DO PANASCAL
QUINTA DA VARGELLAS
Lamego QUINTA DO VESUVIO
Vila Nova da Foz Côa
QUINTA DOS CANAIS

Vila Real

SPAIN

boundary of Douro/Porto wine zone
200m
0   25 kms
0   10 miles

The port country of the Upper Douro valley, Portugal. The leading quintas, or port-growing estates, are marked. The striped area is the port zone; that shaded pink the main vineyard area.

several of the most famous. The best of these bottle their wine in good years and label it with the quinta name. These are junior vintage ports: in really great vintages the produce of the quinta goes into the firm's vintage port, but in moderate to good years they may make a single-quinta wine. These are fascinating as they are from a single estate, like a château-bottled Bordeaux, and being from less august years they mature more quickly than true vintage.

SHERRY

Port starts life as a red wine, sherry as a white. Fortification is carried out later with sherry, after the wine has been made, and the addition of spirit is less central to the taste of sherry. What makes the wine, and what creates the various styles, is the ageing process. Sherry comes in a number of styles, from bone dry to really sweet. Nature dictates the style, at least in part, because some batches of wine (though not all) develop a sort of magic protective blanket once in cask. This covering is *flor*, a layer of special yeast. It develops in some casks, but not others: no-one knows why. The *flor* lends the wine a

yeasty, nutty taste, and it protects it against oxidation — spoiling through too much air contact.

A sherry labelled 'fino' will be a *flor* wine. In Jerez you can buy it unfortified, and in this state it is a wonderfully fresh, pungent and appetising dry white wine. When sent abroad the wine is fortified, which stabilises it but dulls the fino character. Fino should be drunk young and fresh: unlike some sherries, it does not appreciate being kept, either before or especially after the bottle has been opened.

The non-*flor* casks in a sherry bodega will, if left to their own devices, develop into the oloroso style. True oloroso is not sweet, but aromatic and tangy. Most makers blend in some sweetening, darkening wine to produce the style of oloroso their customers want. Amontillado, which is truly an aged fino, is a term used more generally for a medium sherry.

All sherries age in ranks or groups of barrels, called soleras.

To attain consistency, the makers take a proportion of each year's new wine and add it to a cask of the wine from an earlier year. Some of this wine is added to the next-older wine and so on. Each dose of young wine becomes subsumed into the larger mass of older wine. The solera thus establishes a certain style of sherry, and the new wine added little by little adopts that style. Some sherries are bottled direct from the solera (and can be labelled with the solera's name or date of founding) but most are blended from several soleras. Since a solera may well have been established a hundred or more years ago, this can result in bottles with a very venerable date on the label. It is fascinating to speculate on the tiny dash of wine from that long-ago summer contained in the blend.

Good sherry is a fine wine — one of the greats — in terms of character and quality. Finding real quality sherry can be

hard, as most of the wine leaving Jerez is a commercial blend aimed at the tastes of the average drinker. Search out wines which use names such as dry oloroso (as opposed to sweetened), palo cortado (a nutty dry wine), and manzanilla (fino from the sea-coast bodegas). Look also for premium sherries in half bottles: they are better than keeping a half-full bottle for weeks in the hope that sherry can survive this treatment. It can, but it will not show at its best.

OTHER FORTIFIED WINES

Madeira, made on a eccentric island in the Atlantic that is part of Portugal, is forever plotting a comeback. At last, tighter rules about names and labels give it a real chance to re-emerge. The grapes used for Madeira dictate, and denote on labels, the styles. Sercial is very dry, Verdelho medium, Bual sweet and Malmsey sweeter still. However, only wines above about five years old are truly made from these grapes, and the rules now say that the cheaper ones cannot make such a claim. This means that the qualities of true Madeira will come into sharper focus. To appreciate these tastes buy the good stuff, for the ordinary wine (while enjoyable on holiday) cannot stand comparison with other fortifieds. The real madeiras, though, add a wonderful acidity and clean fruitiness to their varying degrees of richness. The dry ones make super apéritifs, the sweeter ones come after dinner or as a mid-morning treat.

Malaga comes from southern Spain, and like sherry is a survival of the medieval taste for warming, sweetened wines. It comes in a range of styles, of which the sweet is the best, and the makers use the solera system as in Jerez.

Elsewhere in the Mediterranean fortified wines are made, and the port and sherry styles have been copied as far away as Cyprus and South Africa. Where fortified wines are of interest, they are dealt with under the country concerned.

Casks being cleaned in the cooperage at the Ferreira port lodge in Vila Nova de Gaia, the Oporto suburb where the port firms are based.

THE MEDITERRANEAN

Vineyard terraces in Cyprus.

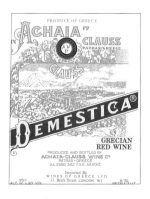

PEOPLE WERE MAKING, trading, enjoying and discussing wine here when the vineyards of the Rhine and Burgundy were still wilderness. Wine began somewhere around the eastern Mediterranean, or perhaps on the shores of the Black Sea. No-one knows for sure. What is certain is that a clear style of wine had developed there by the time of Christ, and wines in this mould are still made today.

The eastern Mediterranean has been something of a back-water for several hundred years: trade and excitement moved west. The wines have stayed stubbornly antique: only in the last few years have Greece and Cyprus, Israel and Turkey, begun to modernise their methods and wine laws. Visitors now find a patchwork of wine styles: supermarkets will have a few wines with familiar grape variety names, many with labels denoting wine areas, more with brand names. Round the corner in an old-fashioned store, people arrive with their own jars to buy country wine straight from the cask. In a few top restaurants, fashionable estate wines in smart bottles will sell at high prices.

Spain or Portugal were not that different a generation ago. There, too, bottled wine was the exception, and strength and sweetness were prized above finesse. Will Greece and the other Mediterranean countries move as fast as the Iberian lands to develop modern wines?

GREECE

Greece, home of the original *grands crus* of the classical world, has plenty of advantages as a wine producer. Hot it may be, but the sea and its cooling breezes is ever-present. Mountains, too, provide cool vineyard sites. The wines that have recently emerged from estates like Château Carras, and from some of the islands, give reason for optimism. Carras was developed from virgin scrub land in northern Greece by a millionaire with dreams of making wine to rival France. With advice from Professor Emile Peynaud, the great Bordeaux expert, Carras makes a range of good-quality red and white wines. As they use French grape varieties and techniques, it is unsurprising that they have a distinctly western style. This is not the only road to quality. As in Portugal and elsewhere, Greece has a vast range of traditional grape varieties — about 300. Some of these have great character and potential for quality. It is hard at present to disentangle which are merely obscure and which deserve to be tried.

Ever-present in Greece is *retsina*, a white wine flavoured with pine resin. This is as much a habit as a preference among Greek drinkers. It is as inexplicable to outsiders as the English love for warm beer. As with the beer, visitors enjoy *retsina* on holiday but find it tastes odd back at home. *Retsina* should be drunk very cold.

Other local heroes have more universal appeal. The Greek islands often make a strong, dark sweet wine which Greeks prize as a pick-me-up at the end of a long, hot day. On Paros it is simply called *mavro* ('black'); on Samos they use Muscat and Malvasia to make both ordinary sweet wines and the well-named Samos Nectar, from sun-dried grapes. Santorini, an eccentric volcanic island, makes a sweet vine called Vissanto; Lemnos has a sweet Muscat. On the mainland, Patras makes the fortified Mavrodaphne.

Straightforward table wines are made everywhere, though some areas have claims to higher than average quality. In the north, they specialise in red wines, with Thrace in the far north-east, and Macedonia inland from the city of Thessaloniki, known for wines from the Xynomavro ('black' again) variety. Further south, in central Greece, whites appear — notably from Zitsa and the Ankialos zone, near Volos. The south, or Peloponnese, offers white wines from the districts of Patras and Mantinia, reds from Nemea. Greece has a wine law modelled on the European norms, with 26 quality wine zones. A useful clue to wine styles is given by seals across the cork: blue is for sweet wines such as Muscats, red for dry wines. Reserve wines have longer ageing; Cava means special, long-aged wines. Many, if not most, bottled wines are sold by the brand rather than the appellation. If you tire of these when on holiday, search out those back-street stores and watch the locals bring their bottles and demijohns to be filled from the cask. Try the wine: it will be unlike anything else, and quite possibly delicious.

CYPRUS

The island of Cyprus follows (in most part) the Greek approach to wine, in so far as the grapes and styles are similar. As in Greece, most of the bottled wine is sold under brand names. The sweet wine tradition is represented by Commandaria: more a legend than actuality, as the mass-produced version of today is a shadow of the intense, sweet wine the Crusaders — and the classical Greeks — used to love. A little authentic Commandaria is still made, but it is hard to find outside its home villages. Straightforward table wines from Cyprus are on the whole pleasant, with most styles represented in the ranges of the big commercial firms. They are more predictable than Greek wines.

TURKEY

Plenty of grapes but not a lot of wine is the story in Turkey. As most of the inhabitants are forbidden wine by their (Muslim) religion, this is understandable. Most of the grapes, perhaps 95%, are eaten as table fruit or become raisins.

The wine is made by large, state-owned companies and private merchant firms and is sold under brand names. Look for Buzbag, and Hosbag; both reds. Villa Doluca is another good red, as are those of the Diren company. Reds wines are better than whites.

THE LEVANT

This rather old-fashioned term suits wine better than the politically-charged 'Middle East'. The Bible is ample evidence that wine was once important here. Israel was the first to move into the modern world, with new vineyards at the end of the 19th century. Lebanon, too, made good wine around this time. A turbulent century of wars and shifting frontiers has not been conducive to vineyards. Fine red wine is made in the Lebanon (this lone star is Château Musar) and good, modern wines on the Golan Heights, between Israel and Syria, and around Galilee. Jordan, Syria, even Egypt have vineyards, but their produce is so far of merely local interest. The wines from this region most often found abroad are Israel's kosher wines.

NORTH AFRICA

French rule made a vast vineyard out of the North African coast in the 19th century, but the last three decades of the 20th have seen the vines shrink as a Moslem population prefers bread to wine. While the great tracts on the plains yield very little wine for export, the occasional bottle from the better hill vineyards does emerge. Tunisia has perhaps the most modern wine industry: there are good sweet whites from Muscat grapes, and the rosé is enjoyable. Algeria, once the biggest producer, has abandoned most of its vineyards. Those that survive include some of the best, rated AOC under French rule and now with the *appellation d'origine garantie* (AOG). Morocco also has an AOG law: zones include the coastal vineyards of Casablanca and Rabat, and the mountain areas of Fèz and Meknès. Red wines can be good: aromatic, rich and long-lasting.

THE AMERICAS

At Oakville in the Napa Valley.

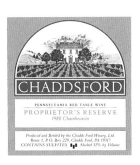

ADD TOGETHER THE ENTIRE WINE production of the Americas, North and South, and you still have less wine than is made in France. But, statistics aside, American wine has in recent years had an enormous influence on what everyone drinks. North America, and in particular the West Coast of the USA, set the technical and philosophical pace for a crucial three decades from 1960 to 1990. A deep gulf opened between the American view of wine and that of Europe. Americans came to grape-growing and to winemaking with an open mind. They planted every kind of vine in a wide variety of places, and when some vineyards prospered they extended them; when others languished they pulled them up. If white wine became more fashionable than red, then vineyards were converted, by grafting, to grow different-coloured grapes. In the winery, too, all was subject to question and change. Chemists and biologists competed to understand and control the age-old processes of winemaking.

The Atlantic gulf was and is exemplified by the names of the wine labels. Early on in California's wine rush, makers found that the grape name was an easy clue to wine style. Chardonnay and Cabernet Sauvignon became synonyms for certain styles of white and red wine. People began to compare one winery's Chardonnay with others. Places and people became known for different styles. The name of the winemaker became interesting information, rather as film buffs follow the fortunes of directors. In France, labels start and finish with a place name: general or specific, a district or a single vineyard, a place. To the French (Alsace excepting), to name a wine after its grape is a gross oversimplification. Ideas have crossed from one side of the Atlantic to the other — in both directions. French *vins de pays* are now often labelled with their grape name. Americans have followed the European example and established a patchwork of appellations — fixed areas of land whose name

can go on wine labels. And both Europe and America, and the world beyond, has moved forward in great leaps in wine technology. What Americans insisted upon was control. There is too much money invested in the Napa Valley for the harvest to be wiped out by bugs, or frost, or mildew. So ways are found to combat the plagues that have beset vines since Noah, and as a result the number of truly bad wines in the world is dropping fast.

The vineyards of North America.

NORTH AMERICA

TWO CULTURES MET AND MINGLED to make North America's winelands. They were the Spanish, exemplified by the Catholic missions and their vineyards, which were essential as sources of sacramental wine, and the northern European, for whose settlers wine was a hoped-for luxury (or in more Puritan quarters a wicked temptation). The East Coast pioneers, French and English, found grapes growing wild in the American woods, but they did not like the taste. Still less did they like the wine these grapes made. The Spanish, in Mexico and later in what is now the USA's South-West, had more luck. Vines of European stock were planted in Mexico in the early 16th century, and thrived. With the slow spread of Spanish influence the vine moved into California in the 18th century. The first adventurers from the USA found vines already growing in Sonoma when they struggled over the Sierras to seek furs and gold in the 1840s and '50s.

The East Coast's winelands were a far harder struggle. Many a time the settlers and their descendants planted European vines. Thomas Jefferson was only the most famous of many thwarted vine-growers. The vines died, some due to the phylloxera louse, others due to extreme heat or cold or humidity.

It was not until the 19th century that winemakers found that hybrid vines would thrive where European ones died. Ohio, New York State and Maryland were but the leading three among the two dozen states with vineyards. Conversely, out west, California, by now part of the USA, began a wine tradition built upon European rather than hybrid vines.

Prohibition put a stop to wine everywhere in North America. It was not until the new prosperity of the post-World War II years that wine became a part of America life — outside, that it, communities which traced their roots back to Italy or Spain and which held on to their wine-drinking habits. The USA is still not a wine country, in consumption terms. Its citizens drink less wine than the British, or the Belgians, or the Dutch, not to mention the Canadians. The Australians drink more than twice as much.

What the USA does have is a very high standard of everyday wine, and an increasing roster of world-class fine wines. The demand for good, interesting wine is large enough, at least in the cities of the East and West Coasts, to support a wide range of wineries and to encourage experiment. In just about every state (there are nine out of fifty with no vines) local vineyards command fierce loyalty. Despite the efforts of other states, American wine means California. The Golden State makes nine bottles in every ten. Most of the wine exported from North America is Californian, though Washington, Oregon and Canada work hard to sell their wines.

CALIFORNIA

As the song has it, California can indeed be cold and damp. Or at least in bits — and those are the parts the wine growers seek out. Most of California is too hot and dry for quality wine. It is on the latitude of southern Spain and North Africa rather than Bordeaux. There are, nevertheless, many thousands of acres of vines in the sweltering Central Valley, where irrigation allows large yields: these grapes become raisins, or go to make basic, if palatable, 'jug' wines.

The quality vineyards are close to the coast, where the quirks of California topography allow cool sea air to flow in among the forested hills. A perfect vineyard in Northern California has cool nights and early mornings due to sea air. It has warm sun to ripen the grapes — but not all day. The ideal is a climate which is just warm enough to prompt ripening of grapes over a long growing season. Growers are still experimenting with different sites and grape varieties to discover what grows best where. Some vineyards have been tried in very cool spots, but have failed to produce really ripe fruit. Those fields are back growing lettuces: the grapes have moved a mile or two further inland.

Because the coast is what makes the climate, it is not too relevant to learn how far north or south the vineyards are. Northern California has the biggest share of quality vineyards, but that is partly because the San Francisco Bay acts as a giant inlet valve for the cool sea air, and partly because many of the pioneer winery owners were urban refugees from the Bay area. Good, cool sites are found as far south as Temecula, between Los Angeles and San Diego.

Opposite: the wine zones of California, Washington and Oregon.

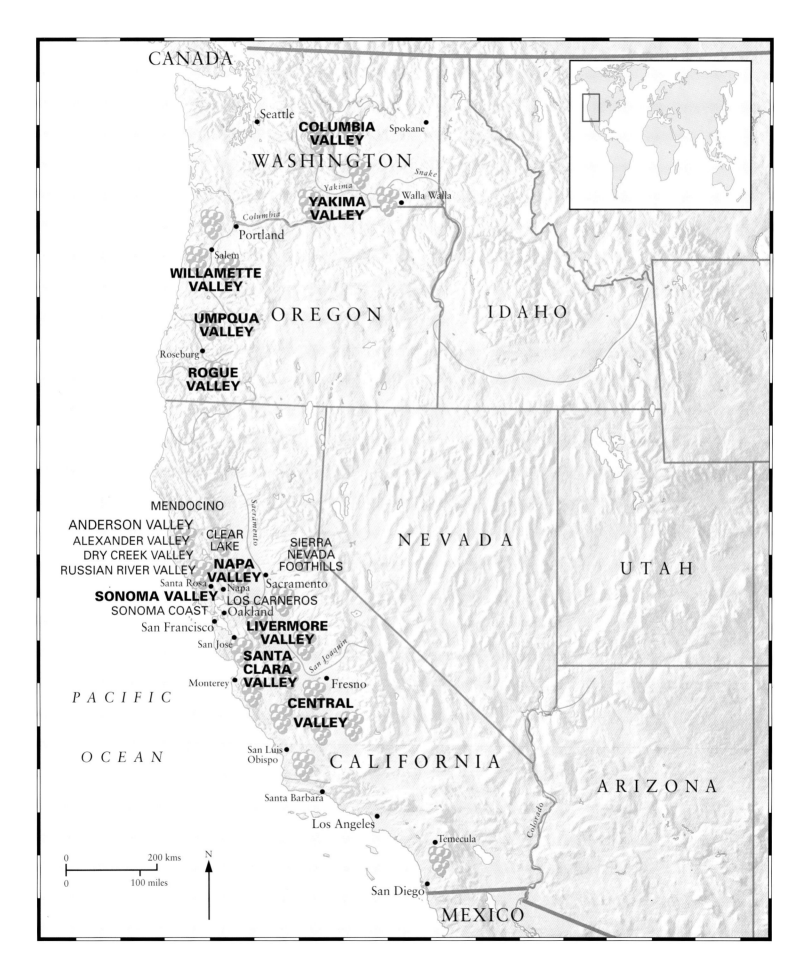

CANADA

Seattle

COLUMBIA VALLEY

Spokane

WASHINGTON

Snake

Yakima

YAKIMA VALLEY

Walla Walla

Columbia

Portland

Salem

WILLAMETTE VALLEY

OREGON

IDAHO

UMPQUA VALLEY

Roseburg

ROGUE VALLEY

MENDOCINO

Sacramento

ANDERSON VALLEY

ALEXANDER VALLEY

CLEAR LAKE

DRY CREEK VALLEY

SIERRA NEVADA FOOTHILLS

N E V A D A

U T A H

RUSSIAN RIVER VALLEY

NAPA VALLEY

Santa Rosa

Napa

Sacramento

SONOMA VALLEY

LOS CARNEROS

SONOMA COAST

Oakland

San Francisco

LIVERMORE VALLEY

San Jose

SANTA CLARA VALLEY

San Joaquin

Monterey

Fresno

P A C I F I C

CENTRAL VALLEY

O C E A N

San Luis Obispo

C A L I F O R N I A

A R I Z O N A

Santa Barbara

Colorado

Los Angeles

Temecula

0   200 kms

N

0   100 miles

San Diego

M E X I C O

complex, age-worthy reds. but wine of just about every style and colour is made there.

Sonoma, over the mountain to the west, is more confusing in its geography. Cool air gets in from the south, via the Bay, and from the north-west, via the Russian River valley. Sonoma's diverse micro-climates mean that almsot any grape can be grown, but there is a certain stress on white grapes for fine sparkling wine, on Chardonnay for well-structured whites, and (in Carneros, which Sonoma shares with Napa) on reds from Pinot Noir.

The other California wine counties include cool, forested Lake and Mendocino in the north with their austere Chardonnay whites and Zinfandel reds; Santa Barbara, with its Mediterranean climate and soft, delicious Chardonnays; Monterey, San Luis Obispo... there are not many corners of coastal California without vines. Inland, the vast Central Valley vineyards make no claim to unique location but they pump out a steady flood of good table wine — far more than all the coast counties combined. Further inland still, some fine sites in the Sierra foothills yield quality wines.

SUMMING UP CALIFORNIA

The experimenting with grapes, with new vineyard sites — and with new breeds of winemakers — goes on. People with no background in wine have bought vineyards and started to make and sell wine with their names on the labels. A sudden rush of dentists, doctors and lawyers — and the odd film star — has descended upon the quiet farmlands of California. With them came wild new ideas about marketing, promotion and business plans.

From the other side of the Atlantic, especially from France, all this looked like dangerous naïveté. Vines are grown where God, and one's ancestors, decided they should be grown. The dictates of tradition are enshrined in law: the *appellation contrôlée* says where and how wine may be made, and where and how it may not. To experiment with different grapes, to plant a vineyard anywhere you like, to alter your methods at a whim: all these things are deeply foreign to the European view of wine. And for anyone except the odd whimsical banker actually to buy a vineyard! Vines were something you inherited, and you tended them the way Papa did before you.

True to type, North America took an elite product — quality wine — and made it democratic.

Napa Valley is a tourist attraction as well as a vineyard.

Just about every grape that can yield wine has been tried in California, but the favourites are the international stars such as Cabernet Sauvignon and Merlot, and increasingly Pinot Noir; and for whites Chardonnay first and a varying clutch of others a long way second. Zinfandel, a red-wine grape, is the state's own. It might, or might not, be Italian in origin, but today it is Californian.

The Napa Valley has the smartest image in California, and the biggest grouping of wineries. The broad valley floor is open to the Bay at the south, so the southern end is coolest, and here (and in adjoining Carneros) they grow Pinot Noir to make excellent red wines. Further north, Bordeaux rather than Burgundy is the spur: Cabernet Sauvignon does well in the Oakville, Rutherford and Stags Leap districts. Here are the most famous wineries, and here the late Baron Philippe de Rothschild joined with Bob Mondavi to make Opus One, California's most expensive red wine. Napa is best known for

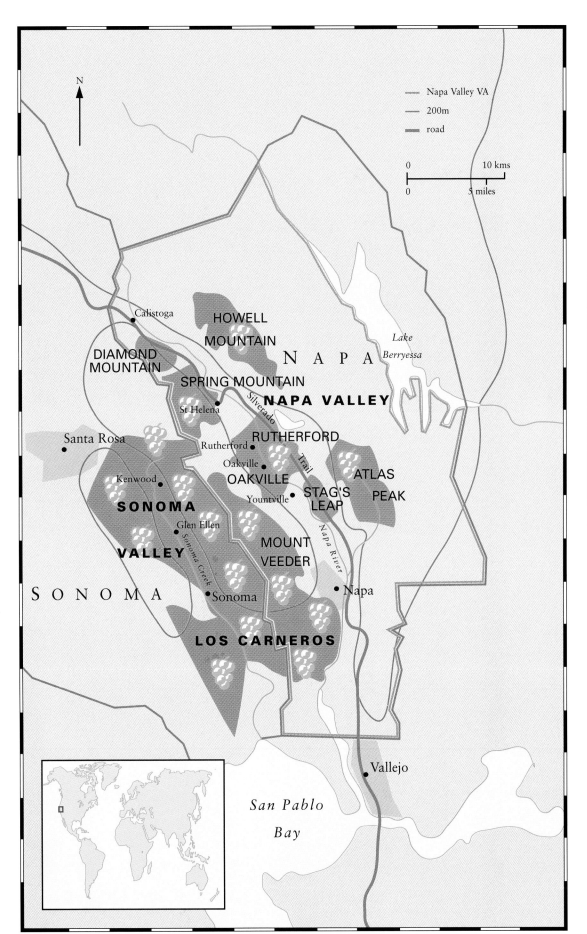

N

Napa Valley VA
200m
road

0   10 kms
0   5 miles

Calistoga

HOWELL
MOUNTAIN

DIAMOND
MOUNTAIN

Lake
Berryessa

N A P A

SPRING MOUNTAIN

St Helena

Silverado

NAPA VALLEY

Santa Rosa

Rutherford

RUTHERFORD

Trail

Oakville

Kenwood

OAKVILLE

ATLAS
PEAK

SONOMA

Yountville

STAG'S
LEAP

Glen Ellen

Sonoma Creek

VALLEY

MOUNT
VEEDER

Napa River

S O N O M A

Sonoma

Napa

LOS CARNEROS

Vallejo

San Pablo

Bay

Above: barrel ageing, as here in the
Napa, is part of the California recipe.
Left: the Napa and Sonoma valleys,
with their Viticultural Areas (VAs).

Next two pages: springtime in Carneros.
Mustard is grown between the vines as a
green fertilizer.

THE PACIFIC NORTHWEST

North of California, the two states of Oregon and Washington make much of their shared latitude with France. Here, they claim, wines of European subtlety and style can be made. As the wine industry only began here in the late 1960s it is too early to judge the truth, but the omens are good. French wine experts have backed their judgement with the purchase of vineyards in Oregon.

Oregon, which is closer to the coast, has a clutch of small-scale wineries offering subtle and sometimes memorable Pinot Noir reds, plus elegant whites from Chardonnay, Riesling and Pinot Gris. Washington, with more vines and larger-scale enterprises, has good clean whites from Chardonnay and a range of other grapes, fruity soft reds from Merlot and Cabernet Sauvignon, and sparkling wines.

THE REST OF THE USA

Up in north-west New York State, a patch of country around a series of lakes offers a partial respite from the biting cold of East Coast winters. Here a major wine industry grew up to slake the thirsts of the eastern cities, using hybrid and native American grapes. Today these wines are still made, but an increasing proportion of the Finger Lakes vineyard region grows European vines, often on small family wineries started in the last 20 years. The same is true of the Hudson River Valley and Long Island, New York State's other quality wine zones. Long Island, in particular, is making red and white wines which confidently challenge Old World classics.

The shores of Lake Erie, both the USA and Canadian sides, have a gentler climate than the rest of the area. Here vines grow, mostly for grape juice, but increasingly for wine. Canada (see below) is setting the pace here.

There are few states on the eastern seaboard, from Maine down to Florida, without at least a patch of vineyard. Most remain purely local, selling their wines from the farm gate. Maryland looks set to make wines of interest, from Chardonnay for whites and Cabernet Sauvignon for red. Florida may have seen the first wine made in North America, from native grapes in 1565, and the tradition is continued today. There are flourishing vineyards in Virginia, along the Blue Ridge Mountains, and in Tennessee.

The big success story of American wine, away from the West Coast, is Texas. From hardly a vine in the 1970s the state shot to fourth in the ranks of wine producers. The tradition is there, with vines grown in Spanish days as far back as 1580. The high plains and hill country of central and north-west Texas are dotted with vineyards, some (appropriately) vast, growing Chardonnay and other white grapes as well as Cabernet Sauvignon and Merlot for red wines. Results are good. Even deeper into the West, New Mexico and Arizona also have their vineyards, though on nothing like the Texan scale.

The Midwest, too, from Michigan across to Missouri, contains hardly a state without vines, though most are hybrids. That said, the wine-loving visitor is sure to be offered a local Chardonnay, Riesling or Cabernet wherever he or she travels in the USA. The only exceptions to the rule are the northern states such as Montana and the Dakotas, where the winters are just too harsh.

CANADA

The USA's northern neighbour has such a snowy reputation that Canadian wines have an unlikely sound. But southern Ontario, beside Lake Erie and along the Niagara peninsula, has just as good conditions for vines as many parts of the USA. The growers do exploit the climate to make large and regular amounts of sweet 'ice wine' — what the Germans call *eiswein* — which is made from grapes frozen on the vine by autumn frosts, a process which reduces their juice to a concentrated sweetness.

Other wines, in a range growing in variety and quality, include reds from Cabernet Sauvignon, Pinot Noir and other varieties, and whites from Riesling and Chardonnay. Such wines are labelled 'product of Ontario': note that wines marked 'product of Canada' can be as much as 75% imported wine.

British Columbia, in Canada's far West, also makes wine in an area which borders the USA's Washington vineyards. White wines, from Riesling, Gewürztraminer and other German varieties, are the most successful here.

Right: the wine zones of the eastern USA and Canada.

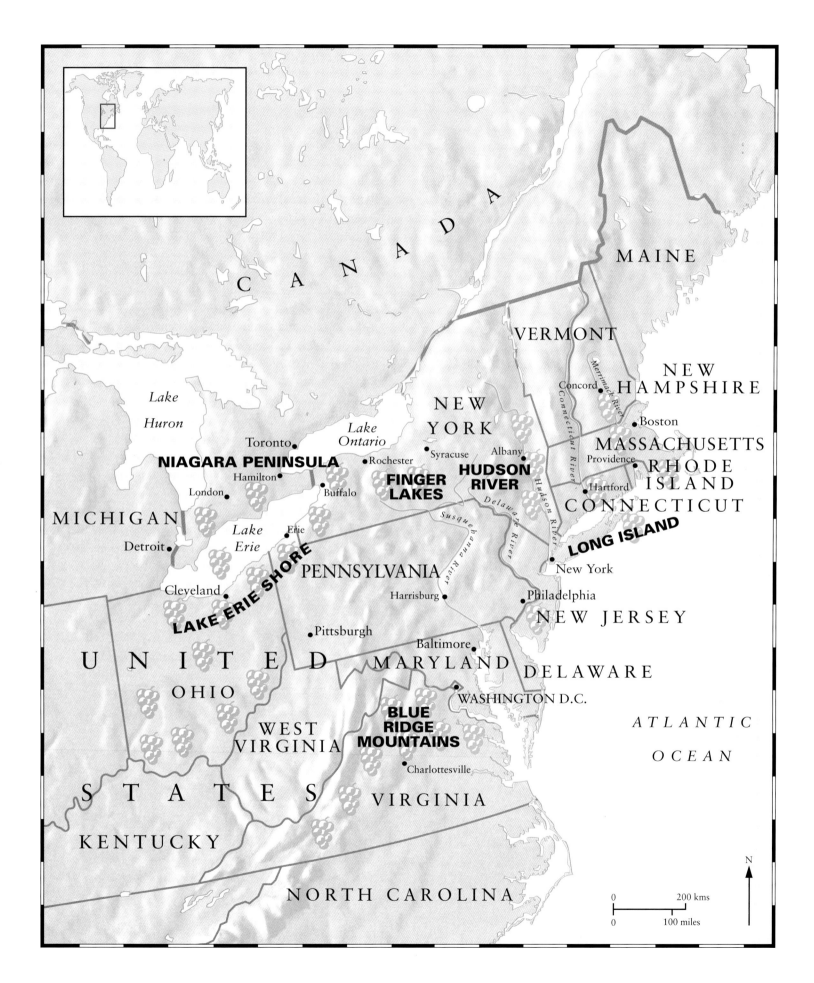

CENTRAL & SOUTH AMERICA

As DESCRIBED ABOVE, MEXICO had the New World's first vineyard and was the springboard for the most successful part of the USA's wine industry, California. Back home in Mexico, however, wine languished in a country where brandy was thought the best use for grapes. Under the Spanish Empire the vines spread south as well us north, and every South American country that has a suitable climate grows grapes for wine. The biggest industries are in Chile and Argentina, though Brazil, too has a flourishing wine trade.

MEXICO

Most of Mexico's grapes make wine for brandy, still the favourite alcoholic drink. But table wine production has seen a revival in the last few years, and some good red and white wines are now being produced. Baja California, the peninsula just south of the California border, is one of the most important wine zones. Here Chardonnay whites and Cabernet Sauvignon reds are made to standards well up to those across the frontier. Elsewhere in Mexico the key to quality wine is height. The vineyards are as much as 7,000ft (2,000m) above sea level to take advantage of cool conditions in this tropical country. Wineries dot the high plateau between the twin ranges of the Sierra Madre. Most wine is still of basic standard, but a few quality-conscious estates, and some of the

Chile and Argentina are the leading wine countries of South America.

mass-production companies, are making good wines, inevitably from the standard repertoire of Chardonnay for white and Cabernet Sauvignon for red. Modest experiments with some Italian and Spanish varieties may point the way towards a Mexican, rather than pan-American, style of wine.

CHILE

Chile is cut off from the world by the ocean, the Andes and (in the north) a desert. Consequently phylloxera, the plague of vineyards world-wide, has been easy to keep at bay. Soils, too, are inhospitable to the dreaded louse, which may be more of a protection than nature's frontiers. Vines are grown un-grafted, on their own root stocks, in vineyards watered by irrigation from the Andes snow-melt. Cool breezes from the sea complement almost unlimited sun. Humidity is low, and so pests and diseases are a minor problem. Few places on earth have such good conditions for growing healthy grapes. All Chile lacked, until recently, was the money and the commercial stability needed to tend the vines and make wine in a way that would harness this potential.

Sporadic exports of superbly flavoursome Cabernet had whetted the appetite of the wine world several times, but always disappointment followed. The next batch of wine would not taste the same: old and dirty casks, poor bottling, all kinds of technical problems added to harm done to trade by the country's endemic inflation. In addition, the local market grew to prefer wines that European and North American tastes found over-old and under-fruity.

Then the late 1980s saw renewed stability, a flood of investment, and a consequent boost to wine quality. The thrilling flavours reasserted themselves. Wineries became export-minded, spurred on by the observed success of Australia in the previous ten years. The foundations were there: along with the excellent natural conditions there was an inheritance of French grape varieties introduced in a previous period of stability in the 19th century.

As a respected British wine importer observed 'anyone with money can invest in skilled people and good equipment. Good climates for growing grapes are rarer. When you have both you are lucky — very lucky.'

Chile has helped its luck along with a sensible new wine law, which provides a framework of regional names, in effect an appellation system on the European pattern. Wine

Vines at Bodegas Trapiche in Argentina.

labelling rules too have been brought into line with Europe. The vineyards, which are found in the centre of the country, north and south of the capital, Santiago, fall into five viticultural regions. These are further subdivided into — working down in size — sub-regions, zones and areas. Wines sold to Europe under the new law will be at least 85% from the place named on the label, though exports to North America and elsewhere may have a minimum of 75%.

The Central Valley, the main wine region, is 200 miles (320km) long from north to south, with Santiago towards the north. It includes several sub-regions, some of which are becoming known for certain kinds of wine. The Maipo Valley has a name for reds from Cabernet Sauvignon and Merlot; Maule, to the south, is a newer sub-region with white wines as its speciality.

Up to the north, the Casablanca Valley has a sea-cooled climate as well as a memorable name: from here come good whites from Chardonnay and Sauvignon Blanc.

Casablanca is part of the Aconcagua region. There are two further regions to the north, where the conditions become progressively hotter and drier. These are Coquimbo, and in the far north, Atacama. Here many vineyards yield table grapes, with wine grapes a minor interest. Some good Muscat wines are made, and there are also fortified wines. The Aconcagua region comes next, with vines in the Aconcagua and Casablanca river valleys: nearly all Chilean wine zones are based around rivers, due to the need for irrigation.

The only vineyards which do not need irrigation are those of the Southern region, in the Itata and Bio Bio valleys. At present these make mostly bulk wine, for local use, but the cool conditions are attracting the attention of winemakers who feel that good white wines may one day come from here.

There is no doubt that Chile has been helped by the familiar names the French heritage of grapes confers: international wine drinkers know what Cabernet Sauvignon and Chardonnay are. The healthy vineyards, the balanced climate and the new techniques offer a recipe for success. The only question lies over the high yields of the Chilean vineyards. With irrigation, the vines can and do produce twice or three times the weight of grapes a European or North American would consider reasonable. Quality and quantity are hard to reconcile in wine, and with the new demand for Chile's wines comes a temptation to overproduce, to sacrifice intensity of flavour for dollars.

Chile has become a worthwhile name to look for in the search for reliable, medium-priced wine. The potential for far better wine is there: one world-ranging Bordeaux expert has said that he expects to make his greatest wine not in France, but in Chile.

ARGENTINA

The legendary thirst of the Argentines currently soaks up most of the large amount of wine made there. Italian influence is strong due to the many colonists from that country: Barbera is among the red grapes, though Malbec (from south-west France) is the main red-wine variety. The reds of Argentina are better than the whites, though new vineyards of European classic vines improve the chances of good whites too in the future. The main vineyard zone is in Mendoza province in the west — not far in distance from the winelands of Chile, though cut off by the wall of the Andes.

This high, cool dry land benefits from irrigation from the Andes. Predictable conditions allow large amounts of good wine to be made at a keen price, especially now winery techniques and equipment are catching up with those of other countries.

Mendoza is not the only wine province in Argentina: the Rio Negro zone to the south, though small, offers attractive cool conditions for white and sparkling wines. San Juan province adjoins Mendoza to the north, and both climate and wines are very similar.

Vines are grown in several other provinces, but none compete in scale with the Mendoza/San Juan wine belt.

International winemakers are starting to work in Argentina, prompted by the ceaseless search for good-quality wine at good prices. They are showing that the calibre of the grapes is very good, and that with expertise and a renewed stress on freshness, a leap in quality can be made.

THE REST OF SOUTH AMERICA

Wine from Peru indeed exists, and it can be good (French advice has been sought and followed). The best vineyards are in the Ica Valley, 200 miles (320km) south of the capital, Lima. The river flows into the Pacific from the high Andes, and the valley has a cool climate despite the tropical latitude. Vines have been grown here for four centuries, since the early days of the Spanish empire. The recent modernisation has yielded some good, and good-value, wines, both white and red, from vines such as Cabernet Sauvignon and Chenin Blanc. Fortified wines are also made in Peru.

Brazil has a big wine industry and exports good-value bottles to North America and Europe. As in Argentina, Italian colonists provided the spur to expansion. Mostly bulk wines are made, often from hybrid vines which do best in the warm, humid climate. Uruguay makes a lot of wine, some of international standard, but drinks most of it it at home. The few bottles which are exported whet the appetite: good, solid reds from the Tannat grape of south-west France are among Uruguay's products. The Andes also allow vineyards in most unlikely places, such as Columbia and Bolivia. Most of the wine they yield is distilled into brandy.

AUSTRALIA & NEW ZEALAND

Vines in the Hunter Valley, Australia.

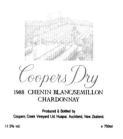

THE SPEED WITH WHICH WINE from these two distant countries conquered Northern Europe's markets amazed both their wine producers (though they were careful to keep an air of nonchalance) and the French. The decade of the 1980s saw Antipodean wine switch from a joke — at home, where beer was king, as well as abroad — to an everyday treat in millions of homes in Britain and elsewhere. French exporters watched in horror as wine-shop shelves gave more and more space to South Australian reds and New Zealand whites.

Australia and New Zealand only needed a wine-appreciating public to prompt a flood of good wine. The climate, the soils and the sites have been known for a century or more. Wine was made in Australia in the 19th century, and it won prizes in Europe, though there was a long gap until the last third of the 20th when quality was not the top priority. As Australia became more cosmopolitan, demand for wine grew.

Australia embraced the new techniques of winemaking, and the scientific approach that went with them. Suddenly, bright, fresh, fruity wines began to appear. While the connoisseurs were appraising California's challenges to top French wines, other wine buyers were discovering Australia and New Zealand's new delights. These fell neatly into the 'good everyday' category, though some are as fine as anything the West Coast, or indeed Europe, can offer.

AUSTRALIA

Most of Australia is too hot and dry to grow vines (or anything else). But the vast continent has ample cool, well-watered vineyard sites. Much exploration is still being done as growers seek out the places where grapes will ripen, but not bake. Australia's wine law is very new, with a thorough-going network of appellations. The new zones, sub-zones, regions and sub-regions brings some unfamiliar names to labels.

Up till now, and still under the appellation scheme, the names of Australia's states have formed the matrix for labelling. New South Wales, in the east, has the great (and thirsty) city of Sydney and a fine range of mountains to provide foothill vineyards. Here are the Hunter Valley, Mudgee and, beyond the range, the vast vineyards of Murrumbidgee, where irrigated land makes oceans of good everyday wine.

Victoria, the country's south-east tip, has famous quality vineyards in (among a score of others) Rutherglen, the Yarra Valley and Goulborn Valley. The Murray River is Victoria's

bulk-wine country. South Australia has flourishing fine-wine zones in the Barossa Valley, Clare and McLaren Vale, and the isolated corner of Coonawarra.

Tasmania, Queensland and (more important) Western Australia all make good wine, but it is the three big eastern states which make the bulk of the wine.

WINE STYLES

Grape variety names allied to those of big wine-producing companies are the traditional key to what is in the bottle. Red wines were the first to become really successful, with Shiraz (the local name for the French Syrah grape) and Cabernet Sauvignon making good, fruity wines which often age well. White wines, from Chardonnay and Riesling, plus Sémillon in a few places, can also be very good.

Much Australian wine is blended from two or more grapes, and from more than one region. An alternative is offered by the increasing list of individual wine estates, where the grapes are grown and the wine is made in the same place, on the French château model. There are now several hundred such estates, and the new wine laws (see above) offer them the chance to call our attention to local styles of wine by the use of appellation names. Australia is in the exciting phase of experimenting with vineyard site, grape variety and technique to discover its own classic wines.

WINE REGIONS

In a country where one winery may make a dozen different kinds of wine, it is hard to generalise about styles and zones. The following are examples of the enormous range.

The Hunter Valley is known for reds from Shiraz and Cabernet, and whites from Chardonnay and Sémillon. Mudgee stresses the same list of varieties, without quite hitting the same heights. Victoria's Goulborn, Grampians and Pyrenees zones offer red wines of style and class. The Yarra Valley has turned its attention to the Burgundian vines Pinot Noir and Chardonnay, which here reach French levels of

Making wine in the Lower Hunter Valley: the Rothbury Estate is one of several modest-sized concerns with an international reputation.

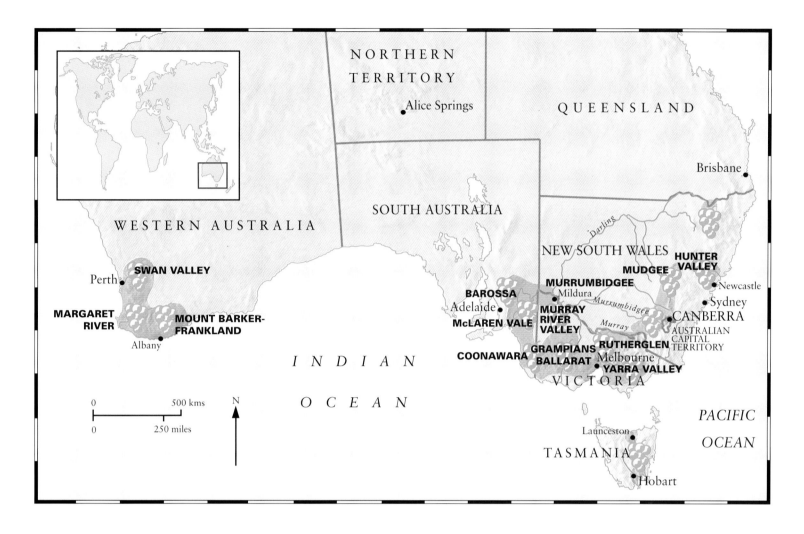

elegance in both still and sparkling wines. Barossa makes fine Shiraz reds, plus Riesling whites. Riesling is more important in the Clare Valley, where fine long-lived red wines are also made. Coonawarra is recognised as the best place in Australia to grow Cabernet Sauvignon. McLaren Vale offers elegant whites from Sauvignon Blanc and Chardonnay, plus good Cabernet reds.

Over in Western Australia, white wines from the Margaret River zone have achieved renown, as have Pinot Noir reds from Mount Barker/Frankland. In this state, more than elsewhere in Australia, the matrix of site, grape and wine style is still being sketched out. The southern island of Tasmania, where the climate really is cool, is seen as the natural home for Pinot Noir to make wines, including sparkling ones, in the Burgundian mould. The results are good, but it is early days.

Fortified and sparkling wines are sometimes overlooked, due to Australia's image as a producer of fruity and enjoyable reds and whites. The investments made by companies from Champagne show that the potential for making good

sparkling wine has been recognised. The classic grapes of Champagne — Chardonnay and Pinot Noir — are widely planted and skilled makers are producing more impressive fizz with each vintage. Fortified wines are a tradition in Victoria, in particular in the Rutherglen and Milawa regions. Delicious Muscats and wines in the style of sherry and port have been made for a century or more, and are still fine value.

The image of Australia abroad is of a bottomless well of good, cheap wine. But Australia is a country of extremes, not least in its climate. Several vintages have been hit by drought, floods, even forest fires. The resulting shortages of wine can mean less choice, and higher prices, in export markets. Vintage variation is becoming a bigger factor in quality wines as vineyards are planted in the cooler zones, which, while they yield better grapes, also face harsher conditions.

Above: Australia's wine zones.
Next two pages: vineyards compete for space with sheep in New Zealand's beautiful landscape.

NEW ZEALAND

Small, distant and inevitably insular, New Zealand came late to wine drinking. Wine was restricted to a minority of New Zealanders of Mediterranean descent, mostly living and farming around Auckland in the north. When the wider public discovered the pleasure, around 1970, a rapid revolution in vineyard technique brought good, even world-class wines within a couple of decades. Some of the best vineyard areas in New Zealand, such as Marlborough in the South Island, are only 20–25 years old.

The ocean moderates New Zealand's climate, and the air and soil are clean and pollution-free. The conditions for growing grapes are well-nigh ideal, especially as the maritime climate generously provides the vines with a long, unstressed growing season. Indeed, some parts can be too cold, and wind stress has been found to be a problem in coastal zones. Shelter belts of trees have solved this problem, but a New Zealand wine farmer is more likely to move the vineyard somewhere else: there are plenty of sites to try.

WINE ZONES AND STYLES

Grapes are grown in both North and South Islands, though there is a concentration of good vineyard zones in the middle of the country, away from both the humid north and the too-cool south. At first, Germany was viewed as the model, both for grape varieties and wine styles. Much Müller-Thurgau was planted — and then dug up again. Recent successes have been with French classic grape varieties. White wine from Sauvignon Blanc, especially from Marlborough, was a great hit in the 1980s, with its combination of crisp fruit and ripe flavours. Chardonnay whites can be good too, with the cool climate lending them personality and style. Red wines are taking longer to perfect, but there are enough good Cabernet Sauvignon and Pinot Noir reds to suggest that they, too, will triumph. Most wines are made to be drunk young: there is no tradition of reds for ageing, though this may change as the vineyards mature and wines gain more structure and depth.

Wine zones are changing fast as new plantings come into production and some old vineyards are torn up. Marlborough, the largest area, is best for white wines, with Chardonnay as well as Sauvignon Blanc doing well. Its sparkling wines have given Champagne experts pause for thought. Hawke's Bay offers good whites, but is perhaps best for reds, including some interesting Cabernet/Merlot blends in the Bordeaux style. Wairarapa is a small, new zone noted for Pinot Noir reds and a range of whites.

New Zealand has some of the most modern and well-run wineries and vineyards in the world, and the overall standard is high. Demand, and some small crops, have pushed prices up, but when reasonably priced these are some of the best of the New World's wines.

The modern wineries of New Zealand, as here at Blenheim, have the latest equipment.

N

0   200 kms
0   100 miles

PACIFIC

OCEAN

*North
Island*

*South
Island*

NORTHLAND
• Whangarei

AUCKLAND

Auckland •
• Te Kauwhata
WAIKATO
• Tauranga
Hamilton •
BAY OF PLENTY

GISBORNE
• Gisborne

TARANAKI
HAWKE'S BAY
• Napier
Wanganui •
• Hastings

• Palmerston North

WELLINGTON
WELLINGTON
Nelson •
• Martinborough
• Blenheim
NELSON

MARLBOROUGH

Christchurch
CANTERBURY

OTAGO

• Dunedin

Invercargill •

*Left: New Zealand's wine zones.
Above: spraying young vines against
mildew.*

THE REST OF THE WORLD

Cape Dutch architecture graces the South African winelands.

THE OTHER WINE LANDS of the world belong to one of two very different traditions. There are the countries where wine is part of Europe's legacy: vines were brought by the colonists and soldiers of the 16th to 19th centuries. And there are the lands of the Far East where wine is indigenous.

As the rest of this Atlas shows, there is little that stands in the way of anyone wanting to make wine except the intractable elements: climate, site and soil. Good advice, modern equipment and reliable grape varieties can be had if the money and will are there. So the world map is constantly sprouting new vineyards as people say 'why shouldn't my country, too, make wine?'

Good viticultural sense would remove vineyards from many of these places, but the desire to succeed against odds — and sometimes local taxes that make imported wine expensive — spur winemakers on. Wine has become a truly international currency. Techniques, fashions and grape varieties traverse the globe. One of the fastest ways to join the world wine mainstream is to hire a 'flying winemaker' — an expert, often Australian, certainly from the other hemisphere, who will make your wine at a season when his own winery is idle. This can lead to predictable wines from odd places, and some fear that wine will start to taste the same, wherever it is made. Climate and soil, though, tend to have the last word.

SOUTH AFRICA

THE DUTCH, AND LATER THE ENGLISH, colonised the southern tip of Africa because it commanded the sea route to the East. Early in the Dutch period, the Governor of the tiny province caused vines to be planted. The Cape of Good Hope was far from anywhere, and it had to be self-sufficient in wine as in much else. Also, wine was needed by ships replenishing on the year-long voyage from Holland to the East Indies. The first Cape wine was made in 1659, making South Africa one of the oldest of the New World vineyards.

What was remarkable about the Cape was not that wine was made — every far-flung European settlement tried, and many succeeded. The Cape went on, within decades, to make a fine wine that became prized by the rich of Europe and which was compared with Tokay. This was Constantia, made by Simon van der Stel, Governor of the Cape, on his farm at Groot Constantia, not far from Cape Town. The first international praise for this sweet dessert wine dates from 1711.

The Cape was lucky too in its settlers. Religious wars in France drove Protestants — the Huguenots — to settle abroad. Some came to the Cape, where the valley of Franschoek ('French corner') was among their early settlements. They brought love of wine and skill at wine farming.

Thus the Cape's wine lands can point to more than three centuries of tradition. Some of the beautiful farms, built in the Dutch style, are owned by descendants of people who settled in these lush valleys in the 17th century.

History aside, the Cape has many advantages as a wine land. The landscape there alternates broad valleys with dramatic mountains. There are slopes of all degrees of steepness, in both sun and shade. There is ample water, often augmented today by irrigation. The sea breezes temper the long hours of African sunshine.

Why, then, has South African not beaten Australia and California in the race for quality among New World wine lands? The answers lie in more recent history. At the start of the 19th century, the Dutch were replaced as colonial

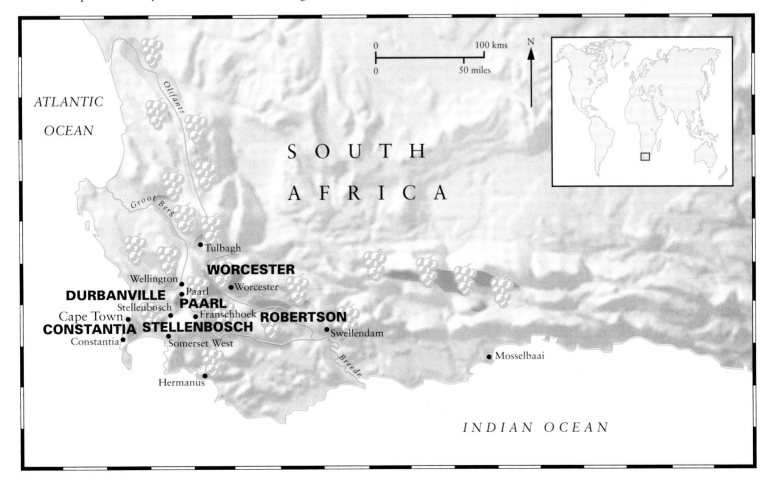

Carved cask in the cellars of Nederberg in the Cape vineyard.

wine as it is sometimes called, is once again to be found on shop shelves in Europe and America.

WINE REGIONS

The lie of the land here is complex, with mountain ranges jostling along the southern coast and jumbling together in the south-west corner of the country. Most of the rivers flow north-west or south-east, forming valleys and ridges which cut across the road inland from Cape Town.

The heart of the wine region lies one valley inland from the coast, around Paarl and Stellenbosch. This is the longest-settled part of the Cape. White-painted farms stand amid tall trees, with vineyards climbing up towards the mountains which turn a dramatic red under the evening sun. As in California, what matters for the wine-growing climate is a clear run for the sea breezes from the south-east.

Paarl and Stellenbosch are the main quality wine zones, dotted with 'estates' — wine farms where grapes are grown and wine made and bottled, on the Bordeaux model. Close to Cape Town is the Constantia district, the starting-point for Cape wine and now with a clutch of ambitious estates, including a revival of the original Constantia wine.

Further north and east, beyond the first mountain ranges, the wide vineyards are mostly irrigated. Here bulk wines are made, with much grape juice still destined for wine for brandy distillation or as grape concentrate. Some pockets of quality wine exist elsewhere: the Hermanus area on the south coast has been proved to have good cool conditions for Pinot Noir grapes. Other areas will certainly be developed as the emphasis switches from bulk wine to more individual bottles.

WINE STYLES

South Africa's first classic, Constantia, was a sweet, probably Muscat, wine. Such wines are still made, though not at such world-beating levels. Fortified wines, in the port and sherry styles, can be excellent: some of the long-matured 'ports', with 40 years in giant wooden vats, attain a delicious chocolate character.

It was not until the 1980s that light wines caught up in quality with the fortified styles. Many years of misguided official quarantine kept classic vine varieties out, putting South African at a disadvantage just when other New World lands were busy copying and surpassing the French prototypes.

proprietors by the British. The vagaries of colonial policy, as run from London, sent wine prices up and down again. Later in the century, Australian vineyards competed for the mother country's market. By the start of the 20th century, South African wine farmers felt that protection was better news than competition. The industry became stifled by controls, which gave farmers a living but which failed to set any premium on quality or innovation. Many South Africans preferred brandy to wine, or beer to both. The country was cut off from outside influences for a crucial decade, the 1980s, and did not see the switch to a wine-loving lifestyle which happened in Australia around the same period.

Change came, however, and a more open regime in the wine industry as in much else allows the chance for South Africa's potential to be realised. South African wine, or Cape

Recent attempts to revive Constantia, at the Klein Constantia estate, have yielded the excellent Vin de Constance.

GRAPE VARIETIES

Much white wine in South Africa still comes from the Steen grape, the local name for the Chenin Blanc of the Loire Valley in France. This adaptable if characterless variety makes good, dry white wine in the Cape, and it is an ingredient in many fortified wines. Sauvignon Blanc has proved a useful grape, as has Chardonnay now that the variety is available. White wines have to be carefully made in this hot climate if they are not to show the blowsy, over-ripe style also found in some Australian wines.

Reds are more likely to show character: the South Africans have their own cross-bred grape in Pinotage, which has Pinot Noir and Cinsaut parentage. It can make excellent mid-range reds, which are complemented by good Cabernet Sauvignons and more recently by Pinot Noirs. The red wines tend to mature quite quickly and to be softer and more fleshy than their European counterparts.

WINE LAWS

Strict labelling laws make South African wine easy to understand. The Wine of Origin system follows normal practice in splitting the country up into regions, districts and wards. There are 13 districts, grouped into five regions. The region most commonly seen on labels is Coastal. If a grape is named on the label, it must comprise at least 75% of the wine in the bottle. The word 'estate' means the wine comes from a farm which uses only its own grapes.

ZIMBABWE

Off the map as far as more august wine atlases are concerned, the high African plains and hills of Zimbabwe do indeed yield wine. The vineyards owe more to politics than environment: a long period of trade sanctions made wine scarce, and Zimbabwe farmers decided to make their own. Their success in winning praise, and even sales, abroad shows that a committed thirst, allied to ingenuity and good techniques, can make wine virtually anywhere. The land is quite high, and therefore cooler than its tropical latitude would imply, but conditions are still not ideal for grapes. Wines are both red and white, with fortified and sparkling wines also made.

ASIA

It was when Indian sparkling wine, made with the aid of expertise from Champagne, appeared in the West in the 1980s that it became widely realised that Asia makes wine. China, Japan, and to a lesser extent India all boast modest and growing wine industries, each making interesting wines both in native and international styles.

CHINA

China has had wine — a small amount, at least — as long as Greece, but it has rarely been popular outside restricted court and cultural circles. Contact with the West via overland trade routes introduced grape vines to Chinese Central Asia, today's Sinkiang province, but now these vineyards yield only raisins.

Modern winemaking in China dates from the missionaries and traders who flocked to the country at the end of the 19th century. French and German missions established vineyards in the province of Shandong, the peninsula that sticks out east into the China Sea south of Beijing. Here the climate is mild enough for vines, and Western joint ventures are having success with Chardonnay and Riesling whites, and Cabernet reds. Other vineyards are north-west of Beijing (where the Emperors once had a famous wine estate), and in the far south near Shanghai, where grapes are grown for a sparkling wine.

Much wine is also made from traditional Chinese grape varieties. These yield drinks in a very different style to the western wines, and are mostly drunk by the Chinese communities of south-east Asia. Rice wine is made not from grapes, but from rice or millet. It is traditional in China.

JAPAN

Most of Japan is unsuitable for grape growing due to the climate: not so much because it is extreme as wrongly phased. Rain falls when it is not wanted, during the harvest, and summer humidity is high. This does not stop the Japanese wanting to make wine, and aspiring to serious quality. Vineyards are mostly on the main, central, island of Honshu, though there are some vines on Hokkaido in the north, and Kyushu in the south.

Many vineyards are of hybrid grapes: the American hybrids, developed on the East Coast of the USA, tolerate Japanese conditions better than do European vines.

The heartland of quality wine in Japan is in the central part of Honshu, west of Tokyo. The Kofu valley, in the district (prefecture) of Yamanashi, was the site of the earliest Japanese vineyards (planted around 700 years ago). Today it is the home of the biggest wine companies, and has vineyards growing European vines such as Merlot and Cabernet Sauvignon for reds and Riesling and Chardonnay for whites. Styles approximate to those of Europe, with good reds beginning to appear, and a famous sweet white in the Sauternes style called Château Lion. Other vineyards with European varieties are found in the neighbouring Nagano province.

Grapes are traditionally grown on high trellises to escape humidity, and many vineyards of this sort still exist. Modern plantations tend to be on the more familiar pattern.

INDIA

India discouraged wine, and indeed all alcohol, until recently, so the vestiges of India's centuries-old wine industry had more or less disappeared. It took a millionaire with western tastes to set things going again, with a sparkling wine made from grapes grown near Bombay. Initially for export only, Omar Khayyam, as the wine is called, is now sold in India. The wine is made using western techniques and Chardonnay is among the varieties used.

Portuguese influence in Goa established vineyards in the same general area 400 years ago, and India had wine well before that; but as in China it failed to become part of the culture. Vineyards survived in the Himalaya foothill provinces, including Kashmir, well into the 19th century.

Today's Indian vineyards are in the hills of the Western Ghats, inland from Bombay. Still as well as sparkling wines are made, with grapes planted including the ubiquitous

Traditional vine trellises in Nagano, Japan. The vines are wrapped up against the winter cold.

Cabernet Sauvignon for reds as well as Chardonnay for the sparkling wine.

OTHER EUROPEAN COUNTRIES

As noted above, it is hard to stop people making wine if it is remotely possible to do so. From this pioneering spirit stem the vineyards of England and Wales, Belgium, the Netherlands and (to an extent) Luxembourg.

LUXEMBOURG

The small country of Luxembourg deserves first place in this list because its wine industry is the biggest of the 'other' countries. It also has more logical reason to exists: the vineyards line the Moselle valley and are a continuation of those of the German Mosel. Indeed, they face some of the German vineyards across the river. Most of the wine is white, and a fair amount of sparkling wine is made. The wines are in a similar style to the German Mosels, with Riesling and Müller-Thurgau among the vines grown. Luxembourg wines are perhaps drier, in the French taste, than most German Mosels. There is a national quality control system similar to that of France. Wines which pass a test can be labelled with the *marque nationale*, and those which pass stricter examinations get to be called *vins classés*.

BELGIUM & THE NETHERLANDS

The Romans grew grapes for wine in what is now Belgium, with the main vineyard area along the Meuse valley. The vineyards suffered from the wars of the 19th and 20th centuries, but were revived more or less from scratch by enthusiasts after the Second World War. Today there are around 100 vineyards in Belgium. Most wine is white, in the same style as those of Luxembourg.

The Netherlands has a handful of vineyards — three at the last count — in the south-east of the country. As in neighbouring Belgium, white wines predominate.

ENGLAND & WALES

Once again, the Romans are credited with the birth of wine in what is now England. After a gap, the vine was reintroduced by the monks, and monastic and other vineyards flourished until the early Middle Ages. Then the English crown's acquisition of Aquitaine, including the wine of Bordeaux,

made it profitless to make wine in England on a commercial scale for three centuries. A few vineyards lingered until the dissolution of the monasteries in the 16th century, but it was not until after the Second World War that English winegrowing began again. The efforts of hobbyists led some hard-headed farmers to appraise the vine as a crop, and by the 1990s the vine was an accepted, if minor, part of the English country scene. There are around 500 vineyards, ranging in size from tiny plots to sizeable estates: the largest has nearly 100 hectares (250 acres) of vines.

Contrary to myth, the English climate, at least in the south-eastern part of the country, is quite dry: there is more rain in Bordeaux. Careful choice of site and soil allows fairly reliable ripening of grapes. Autumn storms are the biggest hazard as the ripening season is long and the harvest late. Most wines are white, from a variety of grapes including Pinot Blanc and Pinot Gris and a wide palette of others. Some red wines are made, and sparkling white wines have been successful.

A few vineyards are to be found in south-east Wales, the driest part of the country; these work to the same pattern as their English neighbours.

Now that the vines in these fairly recent vineyards are reaching full maturity, the British can rightly be proud of a number of excellent native wines; but since the uncertainties of climate means no economies of scale,

INDEX

PICTURE CREDITS

All photographs Cephas Picture
Library.
Photographer Mick Rock, except:
Alain Proust 6, 124; Ryman 11;
Herve Amiard 23, 25; Wine
Magazine 26, 29; Ted Stefanski
32–33, 108–109; Mike Taylor 34;
Nigel Blythe 82, 126; Andy
Christodolo 113